TWO PLAYS ABOUT GOD AND MAN

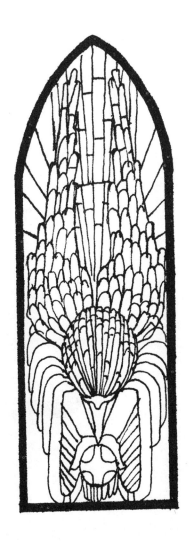

TWO PLAYS
ABOUT
GOD AND MAN

The Devil to Pay
(A FAUSTIAN DRAMA)

He That Should Come
(A NATIVITY PLAY IN ONE ACT)

Dorothy L. Sayers

WITH ADDITIONAL PLANS FOR AMATEUR
PRODUCTION BY MICHAEL WOLFE AND
SCENIC ART BY LUCY AVERY BROOKE

VINEYARD BOOKS, INC.

ISBN: 0-913886-09-2
Printed in the United States of America
Set in Melior type by Printworks, Inc., Norwalk, Ct.
Printed and bound by the Haddon Craftsmen
Book design by Laurel Casazza

Vineyard Books, Inc.
Box 3315, Noroton, Connecticut, 06820

CONTENTS

The Devil to Pay   7

He That Should Come   123

Plans for Amateur Production   187

PUBLISHER'S NOTE

Because we believe that it would have pleased Dorothy L. Sayers, we have included everything that was in the original edition: The list of the first cast, all her prefatory material, and her suggestions for production. (We have also been careful to keep her middle initial as she was known to have strong personal feelings about its inclusion.) In short, we admire Miss Sayers' work tremendously and don't wish to tamper. But because the plays lend themselves so well to amateur production, we have added a completely new section with detailed instructions and plans. Although written with the amateur in mind, these instructions are the work of professionals. It is our sincere hope that the late Dorothy L. Sayers would approve.

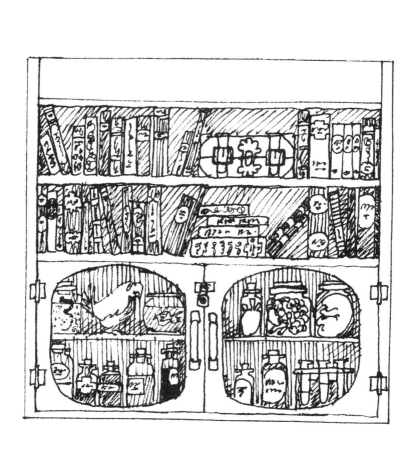

THE DEVIL
TO PAY

Being the famous History of John Faustus the
Conjurer of Wittenberg in Germany; how he sold
his immortal soul to the Enemy of Mankind, and
was served XXIV years by Mephistopheles, and
obtained Helen of Troy to his paramour, with
many other marvels; and how GOD dealt with
him at the last.

A STAGE-PLAY

To the Interpreter
HARCOURT WILLIAMS

"What I have done is yours; what I have to do is
yours; being part in all I have, devoted yours."

Sound without ear is but an airy stirring,
Light without eyes, but an obscure vibration,
Souls' conference, solitude, and no conferring,
Till it by senses find interpretation;
Gold is not wealth but by the gift and taking,
Speech without mind is only passing vapour;
So is the play, save by the actor's making,
No play, but dull, deaf, senseless ink and paper.

Either for either made: light, eye; sense, spirit;
Ear, sound; gift, gold; play, actor; speech and knowing,
Become themselves by what themselves inherit
From their sole heirs, receiving and bestowing;
Thus, then, do thou, taking what thou dost give,
Live in these lines, by whom alone they live.

PREFACE

In my previous Canterbury play, *The Zeal of Thy House*, the problem was to supply a supernatural interpretation of a piece of human history. In the present play, the problem is exactly reversed: it is a question of supplying some kind of human interpretation of a supernatural legend. This means that the supernatural elements in the two stories have called for quite different handling. In the former case, they affected only the moral, and not the machinery, of the fable; take away the visible angels, and the course of William of Sen's fall and repentance remains essentially unaltered. But in whatever way we retell the tale of Faustus, the supernatural element *is* the story. For the "two-hours' traffic of our stage," we must indulge in the "willing suspension of disbelief." We must accept magic and miracle as physical realities; we must admit the possibility of genuine witchcraft, of the strange legal transaction by which a man might sell his soul to Satan, of the actual appearance of the Devil in concrete bodily shape. The Faustus legend is dyed in grain with the thought and feeling of its period; nothing could be more characteristic than its odd jumble of spirituality and crude superstition; of scripture and classical myth; of Catholic theology and anti-clerical humanism; of the adventurous passion for, and the timorous distrust of learning. We may put what allegorical or symbolical construction we like on this fantastical piece of diabolism; but to enjoy it as drama, we must contrive to put ourselves back in spirit to the opening years of the sixteenth century. Accordingly, the better to induce this frame of mind in the spectator, I have deliberately reverted to the setting and machinery of the early Renaissance stage, with its traditional "mansions," its conventional Heaven and Hell-mouth, and its full apparatus of diabolical masquerade.

The picturesque figure of the Devil has a perennial attraction for the playwright, although, theologically speaking, he is apt to make hay of any story into which he intrudes. The fact is, the

Devil is character of very mixed origin; as Mrs. Malaprop would say, he is, "like Cerberus, three gentlemen at once." There is, to begin with, the "fallen seraph" of ancient Talmudic tradition; the rebel created for better things, and suffering torment in everlasting exile from God's presence. It is his dark angelic melancholy that makes the splendour of Marlowe's Mephistopheles and Milton's Satan. Under whatever name he appears, this personage is but one among an uncounted legion of the lost. Although the existence of a chief devil is postulated (whether called Satan, Lucifer, Beelzebub or what not), each evil spirit is conceived of as being a separate personality, rather than summing up in himself the essence of all evil.

Secondly, and inextricably confused, by name and exploits, with the conception of the fallen angels, we have "the Devil"— the absolute spirit of Evil, set over against God, who is the absolute Good. His origin appears to be Persian, and he properly belongs to that dualistic cosmogony which divides the rulership of the world equally between light and darkness, Ormuzd and Ahriman. In Mediaeval theatrical practice, any devil one may choose to bring upon the stage is apt to assume this generalised character of incarnate Evil, whatever references he may make to his diabolic superiors, and however many demonic companions he may summon to his assistance. For the purpose of dramatic symbolism one has to assume that any devil may symbolise "the Devil," and be treated accordingly. Goethe's Mephistopheles has this universality of evil; and in him the poet typifies his own conception of what Evil is, "*der Geist der stets verneint.*"

Thirdly, there is the "merry devil"—a mocking spirit, who probably derives, complete with horn and hoof, from the classical Pan and his satyrs. This lively personage endeared himself deeply to the Mediaeval playgoer, who, in any performance of religious drama, confidently looked forward to the Devil as the "comic turn." Squibs and crackers and poltergeist antics were always part of "Old Hornie's" repertoire; and thus we find the stately Mephistopheles of Marlowe condescending to play vulgar tricks upon the Pope and souse a Horse-courser in a dirty pond. That kind of thing was expected of the Devil, and, had it been omitted from the play, the pit would no doubt have demanded its money back. Trickery and mischief fit in more appropriately with the character of Goethe's Mephistopheles than with Marlowe's; and indeed, towards the end of the long second part of *Faust*, it becomes difficult to remember that the Devil is the father of all Evil; he bears so strong an appearance of being merely an amiable gentleman with a slightly sardonic sense of humour. But indeed, as Marlowe, Milton, Goethe, and every other writer who has meddled with the Devil has discovered, the chief difficulty is to prevent this sympathetic character from becoming the hero of the story.

It is hopeless, at this time of day, to disentangle the stage presentation of the Devil from its inherited inconsistencies, or to make every detail of it fit neatly into a rigid theological system. Nor is it possible to do away altogether with the inherent unreason that attends the practice of Art Magic. If, as we are so often told, religion and magic were formed out of the same raw material, nothing could be more remarkable and impressive than the difference, in the finished article, between the rational severity of the one and the incoherent irrationality of the other. It must be remembered that the Mediaeval magician did not, generally speaking, set to work to call up devils in the name of Beelzebub; he called them up in the name of the Trinity. However sordid, vile or ridiculous the end for which he summoned the spirits, the ultimate sanction invoked to attain that end was the power of God and His angels. In the very act of denying and defying God, he surrounded himself with every protection that the name of God could afford against the consequences of the act. In their more blasphemous excesses, his conjurations were spells, explicitly compelling God, by the power of His own name, to perform the conjurer's will. It is this curious dissociation of the power from the source of power that characterises magic as opposed to sacrament. The magical power is, in fact, considered to inhere in the divine name itself, and to operate automatically and independently of the divine authority. Thus the ancient manuals of conjuration present us with the somewhat inconsequent spectacle of a magician urgently calling upon God to protect and assist him in the carrying-out of such agreeable little bedevilments as the diseasing of his neighbour's cattle, the debauching of his neighbour's wife, or even the consort and enjoyment of delectable she-devils in bodily form. Whether, indeed, a generation so addicted as our own to the cherishing of mascots and the reckless abuse of ideological formulae is enti-

13

tled to cast the stone of scorn at its Mediaeval forebears is matter for consideration.

But when we have allowed for all its fantastical trappings and illogical absurdities, the legend of Faustus remains one of the great stories of the world; a perpetual fascination to the poet, whose task it is to deal with the eternities. For at the base of it lies the question of all questions: the nature of Evil and its place in the universe. Symbolise Evil, and call it the Devil, and than ask how the Devil comes to be. Is he, as the Manichees taught, a power co-equal with and opposed to God? Or, if God is all-powerful, did He make the Devil, and if so, why, and with what justification? Is the Devil a positive force, or merely a negation, the absence of Good? In what sense can a man be said to sell his soul to the Devil? What kind of man might do so, and, above all, for what inducement? Further, what meaning are we to place upon the concept of hell and damnation, with which the whole concept of the Devil is intimately bound up?

Questions such as these are answered by every generation in the light of its own spiritual needs and experience. And for each writer, when he has determined his own interpretation of the central mythus, there is, of course, the added technical interest of discovering how many features of the original legend offer themselves as valuable factors in his system of symbolism.

In the true spirit of the Renaissance, the legendary Faustus sells his soul for the satisfaction of intellectual curiosity and the lust of worldly power. Marlowe accepts those inducements as valid, and, though his sympathies are very much with Faustus, does not shrink from the tragical end of the story. Faustus is damned in accordance with the terms of the bond, and the sombre close of the drama is unrelieved by any ray of hope. In this play, there is scarcely any trace of the conventional Mediaeval hell of physical fire and brimstone; the famous speech of Mephistopheles embodies a purely spiritual concept of damnation:

> "Why, this is hell, nor am I out of it.
> Think'st thou that I, who saw the face of God
> And tasted the eternal joys of Heaven,
> Am not tormented with ten thousand hells
> In being deprived of everlasting bliss?"

For Goethe, it was impossible to accept the idea that desire for knowledge could be in itself an evil thing. Though Faustus signs the bond, Mephistopheles is cheated in the end, and Faustus goes to Heaven. This game of cheat-the-devil is in full accordance with the spirit of the early moralities; these often finish with a judgment scene, conducted by Our Lady in the strictest legal form, in which the Devil is tripped up over the terms of a compact, rather in the manner of Shylock in *The Merchant of Venice*. Goethe conceives of the Devil as a necessary part of God's plan for the world: he is the power "*der reizt und wirkt und muss als Teufel schaffen.*" The deadly sin is to give up striving and rest content, and the Devil is the irritant that keeps man at work. Goethe's Faust learns to use his infernal power to a good end, and finds contentment only in devotion to the service of man. It is while busily engaged in a work of public usefulness that he finds himself ready to say to the fleeting moment: "*Verweile doch, du bist so schön*"; and the comment of the angels is:

> "*Wer immer strebend sich bemüht*
> *Den können wir erlösen.*"

To endeavour to do again what greater poets have already magnificiently done would be folly as well as presumption; and I have tried to offer a new presentment of Faustus. All other considerations apart, I do not feel that the present generation of English people needs to be warned against the passionate pursuit of knowledge for its own sake: that is not our besetting sin. Looking with the eyes of to-day upon that legendary figure of man who bartered away his soul, I see in him the type of the impulsive reformer, over-sensitive to suffering, impatient of the facts, eager to set the world right by a sudden overthrow, in his own strength and regardless of the ineluctable nature of things. When he finds it is not to be done, he falls into despair (or, to use the current term, into "defeatism") and takes flight into phantasy.

His escape takes a form very common in these times: it is the nostalgia of childhood, of the primitive, of the unconscious; the rejection of adult responsibility and the denial of all value to growth and time. Time has been exercising the minds of many writers of late. It has been suggested that it is pure illusion, or at most a cross-section of eternity, and that we may be comforted for the failures of our manhood by remembering that the youth-

15

ful idealists we once were are our permanent and eternal selves. This doctrine is not really even consoling; since, if our youth is co-eternal with our age, then equally, our age is co-eternal with our youth; the corruptions of our ends poison our beginnings as certainly as the purity of our beginnings sanctifies our ends. The Church has always carefully distinguished time from eternity; as carefully as she has distinguished the Logos from the Father. It is true that we must become as little children and that "except a man be born again, he cannot see the kingdom of God." But that is not to be done by attempting to turn time backwards, or deny its validity in a material universe. "How can a man be born when he is old? Can he enter the second time into his mother's womb and be born?" The answer is that he cannot. "That which is born of the flesh is flesh, and that which is born of the spirit is spirit." Time and eternity are two different things, and that which exists temporally must admit the values of time. Against the exhortation to take refuge in infantilism we may set the saying of Augustine of Hippo concerning Christ: "*Cibus sum grandium; cresce et manducabis Me*"—"I am the food of the full-grown; become adult, and thou shalt feed on Me."

Has Evil any real existence, viewed *sub specie aeternitatis*? I have suggested that it has not; but that it is indissolubly linked with the concept of value in the material and temporal aspect of the universe. It is this issue which Faustus refuses to face; rather than grapple with the opposition of good and evil, he dissociates himself from common human experience. The results to his soul of this attempt to escape reality are displayed in a final judgment scene, where (with a rigid legal exactitude which, I feel sure, the Mediaeval mind would heartily approve) the Devil is cheated of his bond, but receives his precise due. The notion of the Devil as being set in charge of the place of purgation, as well as of the place in which all evil is consumed, was familiar enough to the Middle Ages, as is clearly seen in the Wakefield Pageant of *The Harrowing of Hell*, where Christ rebukes Satan in the words:

"I make no mastry but for myne,
I wille theym save, that shalle the sow
Thou has no powere theym to pyne,
Bot in my pryson for thare prow [profit]."

Of the original Faustus legend, certain episodes are reproduced in some form or another in practically all treatments of the subject: Faustus' raising of Mephistopheles; his "disputations" with him concerning the nature of God; his twenty-four years' bond to Hell; his journeys to Rome, where he plays tricks upon the Pope, and to the Court of Charles V, where he assists the Imperial armies to achieve their victories in Italy; his having Helen of Troy for his paramour; and the final scene in which the Devil comes to claim his own. His servant, Christopher Wagner, is also traditional. One version recounts how Faustus sought to marry "a beautiful servant-girl," but was prevented by Mephistopheles, on the ground that marriage was a sacrament, and therefore an action pleasing to God and contrary to the terms of the bond. This episode forms the basis for the First Part of Goethe's *Faust*.

The central part of the story is chiefly taken up with a long series of disconnected marvels and miracles, mostly of a purely mischievous and puckish sort, as when Faustus swallows a wagon of hay and a span of horses, makes flowers bloom at Christmas, cuts off his own leg and restores it, draws wine from a table, or attends the Pope's banquet invisible and beats the guests about the head. None of this episodic material offers much opportunity to the dramatist for anything but "inexplicable dumb show and noise"; it is the beginning and the end of the tale that constitute its eternal appeal. In a version designed to be played in the restricted period of an hour and forty minutes, it has been necessary to exclude all merely episodic matter, and to concentrate on those incidents which are capable of being compressed into a reasonably coherent dramatic structure.

What Tophet is not Paradise,
what Brimstone is not Amber,
what gnashing is not a comfort,
what gnawing of the worme is not a tickling,
what torment is not a marriage bed to this damnation,
to be secluded eternally, eternally, eternally,
from the sight of God?

JOHN DONNE
Sermon preached to the Earle of Carlisle.

The Devil to Pay was originally produced in the Chapter House at the Canterbury Cathedral Festival, 10–17 June, 1939, under the management of the Friends of Canterbury Cathedral, with the following cast of professional and amateur players:

WAGNER	Philip Hollingworth
LISA	Betty Douglas
FAUSTUS	Harcourt Williams
MEPHISTOPHELES	Frank Napier
CARDINAL	Charles Reeves
PRIEST	William Fordyce
POPE	Geoffrey Keable
HELEN OF TROY	Mary Alexander
YOUNG FAUSTUS	Alastair Bannerman
AZRAEL	Stanley Pine
EMPEROR	William Fordyce
EMPRESS	Vera Coburn Findlay
CHANCELLOR	Sidney Haynes
SECRETARY	Marshall Hughes
SOUL OF FAUSTUS	Max Wood
JUDGE	Raf de la Torre

DEVILS: Nigel Beard, Michael Foster, Anthony Ware, John Williams.

CITIZENS: Paddy Finn, Kathleen Hetherington, Rachael Hubble, Maud Lister, Joan Pollard, Eileen Shipp, Frank Kipps, Howard Overy, Edgar Parker-Pope, Jack Vane.

COURTIERS: Frank Kipps, Jack Vane

PAGE: Donald Foster.

LADIES: Paddy Finn, Rachael Hubble.

The Music for the Songs and Final Chorus composed
by GERALD H. KNIGHT
Singers
String Orchestra
The Play produced by HARCOURT WILLIAMS
Scenery, Lighting and Stage Effects by FRANK NAPIER

19

The Devil to Pay was first presented in London by the Daniel Mayer Company Limited at His Majesty's Theatre on July 20th, 1939, with the following cast:

WAGNER	David Phethean
LISA	Diana Deare
FAUSTUS	Harcourt Williams
MEPHISTOPHELES	Frank Napier
CARDINAL	Frank Woolfe
PRIEST	Alexander Archdale
POPE	J. Fisher White
HELEN OF TROY	Mary Alexander
YOUNG FAUSTUS	Alastair Bannerman
AZRAEL	John Munn
EMPEROR	Ernest Clark
EMPRESS	Betty Douglas
CHANCELLOR	Frank Woolfe
SECRETARY OF STATE	John Lalitte
JUDGE	Raf de la Torre

FOUR DEVILS: Kevin Keogh, Peter Scott, Peter Graves, Marshall Haley.

PAGE: John Wilson.

CHOIR: Grace Nevern, Peggy Hale, Rae Allan, Gwen Bateman, Betty Douglas, Alexander Archdale, Philip Merritt, Reginald Thurgood, John Lalitte, Murray Davies, Edwin Hill.

Citizens, Courtiers, Ladies, etc., from the members of Choir.

The Play produced by HARCOURT WILLIAMS

PERSONS OF THE DRAMA
in the order of their appearing

CHRISTOPHER WAGNER, Famulus to Faustus
LISA, Maidservant to Faustus
JOHN FAUSTUS, a Conjurer
MEPHISTOPHELES, an Evil Spirit
A CARDINAL
A PRIEST
THE POPE
HELEN OF TROY, a Magical Apparition
JOHN FAUSTUS, in the body of his transformation
AZRAEL, Angel of the souls of the dead
THE EMPEROR
THE EMPRESS
A CHANCELLOR
A SECRETARY OF STATE
THE SOUL OF JOHN FAUSTUS
THE JUDGE
Devils, Citizens, Courtiers, Ladies, etc.

SCENES

I—Wittenberg: Faustus' Study, 1502
II—Rome: The Forum, 1503
III—Innsbruck: The Emperor's Court, 1527
IV—The Court of Heaven: Eternity

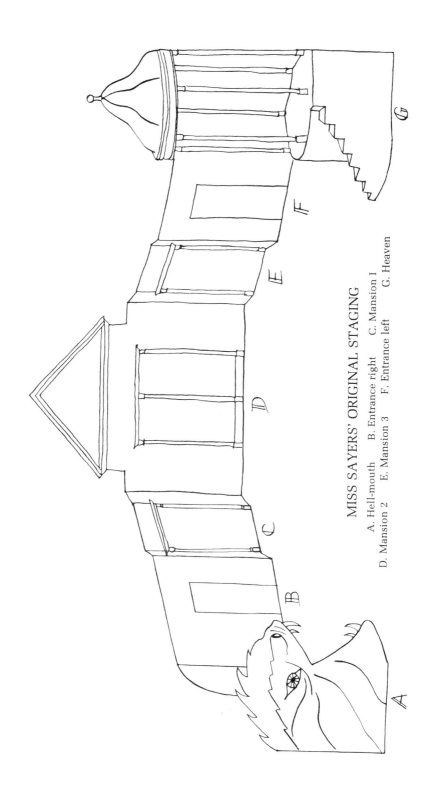

MISS SAYERS' ORIGINAL STAGING

A. Hell-mouth   B. Entrance right   C. Mansion I   G. Heaven
D. Mansion 2   E. Mansion 3   F. Entrance left

SCENE I (Mansion 1)

Wittenberg—Faustus' Study

{*Lighted candles right and left in sconces. Centre, tall mirror covering entrance to Mansion 2. Left, big chart hung on rollers, showing eclipse of the sun. Right back, between Mansions 1 and 2, trick shelf with bottles, etc. On right wall, stoup of Holy Water. Left centre, chair, and table with books, parchments, flasks and other alchemical and astrological apparatus, together with a wax taper. On floor, down centre, a double circle and pentacle in white chalk. Enter from Mansion 1, WAGNER, carrying a lighted lantern, a long sword, a glass jar, five small lamps tied together, a cabbage and a dried stockfish, and reading a large book by the light of the lantern.*}

WAGNER

Oh, dear! Oh, dear! I shall never be ready in time. Lisa!
Lisa! (*shuffling to table*). So much to do since my master gave
up theology and took to astrology and physic. "Ioth, Aglanabroth, El, Aniel, Anathiel, Anazim"—what terrible great
hard words! (*Sets down lantern, dropping cabbage.*) Alas! what's
that? Oh, it's only the cabbage. (*Grovels for it, dropping sword.*)
Heaven be praised! I thought it was the precious Holy
Water. (*Stands clutching all his parcels and holding book close to
lantern.*) "Craton, Muriton, Agarion, Pentessaron"—Bless
me! I have forgotten the mandrakes—no, I remember, I put
them in my pocket. (*Attempts to verify the mandrakes, dropping
stockfish.*) Lisa!
   {Enter LISA, left.}

LISA

Oh, my poor Wagner! How dreadfully burdened you are.
Here, let me take some of those things. (*Picking up stockfish.*)
What's this for? Friday's dinner?

23

WAGNER

It's a present from the poor fishmonger whose horoscope we cast free of charge. And this cabbage is from the old peasant we cured of the itch. I do hope I've got everything.

LISA *(putting fish and cabbage in her apron)*

I'm sure you have quite enough.

WAGNER

This is a flask of Holy Water from the River Jordan itself. Set it on the shelf. Carefully. It has been blessed by the Pope. And you must take these lamps and fill them with the very best consecrated oil. I'll put the Doctor's sword over here.
     {*Wanders away, still clutching book, and leans sword against wall, right.*}

LISA *(setting flask on shelf)*

Were there many at his lecture to-night?

WAGNER

Yes, a great many. But I'm sure the most part of them care nothing for the brave things he tells them about Gemini and Capricorn and the movements of the planets. They only want to learn how to get rich, or to beg him to cure their diseases. There was a whole rag-tag and bob-tail besieging him at the door. In his place I wouldn't be troubled with them.

LISA

He is so kind. He will always help them if he can. He can't bear to see any one suffer *(at table, collecting lamps)*.

WAGNER

So he sent me on ahead to prepare the room for him. We are to do great things to-night. Don't take the lantern.
I need it to study my book.

LISA

But all the candles are lit.

WAGNER *(astonished)*

So they are! I didn't notice. *(Importantly.)* But then, I'm so very busy. Now where in the world did I put the chalk? I'm sure I had a piece somewhere.

LISA

I expect it's in your pocket.

WAGNER

I believe you're right. What a clever girl you are, Lisa, and so very, very pretty.

LISA

Foolish Wagner!

WAGNER

Don't you think you could call me Christopher? *(Pleadingly.)* It isn't a bad name. Do please try. It would make me so happy. I'm very fond of you, Lisa.

LISA

Foolish Christopher *(skipping nimbly out of reach).* Now, you mustn't waste time. Find your chalk and get on with your work, or you won't be ready when Dr. Faustus comes.

WAGNER

The chalk? Yes, I'm sure it's here, but it seems to be mixed up with something. *(Pulling bundle of roots from his pocket.)* Of course—the mandrakes. They must be hung in the chinmey to dry.

LISA

What strange-looking things! Put them in my apron. *(He tries to kiss her; she holds the lantern between them.)* Now, be a good Christopher and study your great book.
{*Exit, left, with lantern and lamps.*}

WAGNER *(looking after her)*

Sometimes I think she doesn't take me seriously. Well, I must get on. *(Kneels and writes in circle, book in hand.)* The anagrams of God in the five points of the pentacle. IHS, El Ya, Alpha, Omega. So. And the names of God between the points. Adonai. Emmanuel. Panthon. Tetragrammaton. Messias. So. And between the lamps in the circle, five signs of the Cross. One, two, three——
{*Re-enter LISA, with lamps.*}

LISA

I have filled the lamps. What are you writing there?

WAGNER

Ah, that is a secret. Give them to me—so, one at each point of the star. These are high and mighty matters, and not for girls to know about. It's all written in this book, that was given to Dr. Faustus by the great conjurer, Cornelius Agrippa. To-morrow, we shall be richer and more powerful than the Emperor. We shall have spirits to fetch and carry for us——

LISA

What? You will not . . . He doesn't mean to . . . Oh, Christopher! There will be no danger to Dr. Fuastus?

WAGNER

Of course not. No danger can pass this circle. Besides, I shall be there to protect him. How brave it will be! We shall be masters of all the treasure in the world. We shall heal all the

troubles of mankind with a wave of the wand. We shall
prank ourselves in costly apparel, and you and I will be
married, Lisa, and fly to the court of the Grand Cham on
the back of a winged basilisk. Tell me, dear Lisa, tell me——

LISA

I hear the Doctor coming.
> {Enter FAUSTUS, Mansion 1. He wears a great cloak over his
> doctor's gown. LISA runs to greet him.}

Oh, sir! how late you are! And how wet! Give me your
cloak. I'm sure you must be tired to death. Sit down and
rest. I will have a fine hot supper ready for you in a moment.

FAUSTUS

Thanks, Lieschen, thanks. But I shall need no supper. I have
work to do.
> {Takes off his cloak and doctor's cap. LISA hangs them up.}

LISA

No supper! Why, you have eaten nothing all day.

FAUSTUS

My work must be done fasting. (He sits on a chair.) Bring me
a bowl of water, and the robe, slippers and girdle you will
find in my chamber. Is everything ready, Wagner?
> {Exit LISA, left.}

WAGNER

Yes, sir. I have this moment finished the circle.

FAUSTUS

See that it is accurately drawn. One of your spelling mis-
takes, or a touch of your usual absent-mindedness, might
land us both in a very queer place. (WAGNER, alarmed, checks
all his hieroglyphics again by the book.) Oh, God, I am sick at
heart. When I see how ill this world is governed, and all the
wretchedness that men suffer, I would give my immortal
soul to be done with it all.

WAGNER (crossing himself)

Heaven forbid. What a thing to say! When you think how
easily your immortal soul might go wriggling away through
a gap in the circle, like a rabbit through a fence. Or my soul,
for that matter.
    {He carefully touches up a point of the pentacle.}

FAUSTUS

Don't be alarmed. You will be safe enough if you stay where
I put you and don't lose your head and run away.
    {Re-enter LISA with slippers, bowl and napkin. She puts the bowl
    on the floor while she removes FAUSTUS' shoes and puts on his
    slippers.}
That will do. Leave it to me. I see you have drawn out the
figure of the sun's eclipse.

WAGNER

Yes, sir. But I don't altogether understand it. The moon
gives light to the earth. Why then do we see her black?

FAUSTUS

The moon has no light of herself. When she passes between
the earth and the sun she shows but as a mass of dark
matter, as your head does, between me and that candle.
    {He washes his hands in the bowl LISA holds for him.}

WAGNER

I see. And if the sun were to pass between us and the moon,
would he show dark also?

FAUSTUS

No; for he is the very source of the light, and in him is no
darkness at all. My robe and girdle, Lieschen.

LISA

Oh, sir! I don't like the look of that robe, and the girdle with
all the strange words upon it. They are too much like what
you have there upon the floor. I am afraid of them. Will you

28

not sit and have your supper like a Christian, and leave
these fearful conjuring tricks to ignorant, unhappy men who
know no better?

FAUSTUS

What is all this? Have you been talking, Wagner?

LISA

What do you need with riches and power and the court of
the Grand Cham, and wicked spirits and basilisks—you that
are happy in your great wisdom and learning?

FAUSTUS

Child, the greater the wisdom, the greater the sorrow. The
end of all our knowledge is to learn how helpless we are.
Divinity, philosophy, astrology—I have studied them all.
There are no springs of comfort in that barren desert of doctrine. Physic but lays a patch to the old garment; the stuff
itself is rotten, warp and woof; the corruption eats deeper
than our drugs can reach. (Violently.) What is this folly about
riches and worldly delights? Do you think I care for such
toys? But if magical power can aid me to resolve the mystery
of wickedness, lay bare the putrefying sore at the heart of
creation, break and remake the pattern of the inexorable
stars—I have frightened you. Fetch me my robe, and do
not meddle with what you cannot understand. There,
I know you mean well, but do not vex me now.
    {Exit LISA, left, removing bowl and shoes.}
Wagner, why do you not attend to your work, instead of
chattering to Lisa?
    {Takes off his gown and lays it on the chair.}

WAGNER (hurt)

I have worked very hard indeed. I have purchased the
lamps, ordered the oil, taken your sword to be ground,
brought home the Jordan water, finished the circle and
learnt a great many very long and difficult names out of
this book. I hoped you would be pleased with me.
    {Re-enter LISA with robe and girdle and puts them
    on FAUSTUS.}

FAUSTUS

Why, so I am. You are an honest, industrious fellow—and if your heart is a better organ than your head, it was not you that had the making of them. Thank you, child. Now run away, and never trouble your pretty head about us. And remember, no matter what you may hear, you must not cross the threshold of this room to-night. On no pretence whatsoever. Do you hear me?

LISA

Yes, sir. May God and His holy angels protect us all.
{Exit, left, taking FAUSTUS' gown.}

FAUSTUS

Now, Wagner, to work! Bring the book to me.

WAGNER

(bringing stoup across from wall and giving it to FAUSTUS)
This is empty. Will you have the blessed water from the Jordan?
{He lays the book on the table.}

FAUSTUS

Yes. But make haste; for this spirit will not come save he be called between the ninth hour and midnight.
{WAGNER brings flask and fills the stoup which FAUSTUS holds.}

FAUSTUS (signing the water)

In nomine Patris et Filii et Spiritus Sancti, exorcizo te, creatura aquae, ut fias aqua exorcizata ad effugandam omnem potestatem inimici. Amen.

WAGNER

Amen.
{While WAGNER puts back the flask and changes it by means of the trick shelf, FAUSTUS sprinkles the water within the circle.}

FAUSTUS

Asperges me Domine hyssopo et mundabor, lavabis me et
supra nivem dealbabor. Gloria Patri et Filio et Spiritui
Sancto.

WAGNER

Sicut erat in principio et nunc et semper et in saecula
saeculorum. Amen (He puts back the stoup and now brings the
sword, naked, to FAUSTUS, who has meanwhile taken the book from
the table and opened it.) Must I put out the lights, Master?

FAUSTUS (examining the circle)

Put them all out, and bring me a lighted taper.

WAGNER (takes taper from table, lights it at one of the
candles, and then extinguishes the lights)

Oh, Master, it's going to be very dark and not at all com-
fortable. I don't think I care very much about being rich
and powerful and riding on b-b-basilisks. D-d-don't you
think it would be better to stop all this, and have a nice
little astrology lesson or something?

FAUSTUS

Take courage, Wagner. Thou wilt not desert me now? There
must be some meaning in this tormented universe, where
light and darkness, good and evil forever wrestle at odds;
and though God be silent or return but a riddling answer,
there are spirits that can be compelled to speak.
    {WAGNER returns, carrying the taper.}
Now follow me into the circle, and see that thou close it
well after we have passed over.
    {They step into the circle through a gap left in the figure, which
    WAGNER closes carefully with chalk.}
Light the lamps.

WAGNER

My hand trembles. (He lights the lamps.) Oh, dear! what will become of us? Ugh! Something brushed past my face, like a bat. Would I were well out of this.

{*He extinguishes the taper.*}

FAUSTUS

Be silent. Stand back to back with me and be sure you let neither hand nor foot stray beyond the circle. Now we begin.

In the name of the most high God, maker of Heaven and earth and of all things under the earth, Ioth, Aglanabroth, El, Abiel, Anathiel, Amazim, Messias, Tolimi, Ischiros, Athanatos, I require of Thee, O Lord, by the seal of Solomon and by the ineffable name wherewith he did bind the devils and shut them up, Adonai, Aglai, Tetragrammaton, grant me Thy virtue and power, to cite before me Thy spirits which were thrown down from Heaven, and in especial that spirit which is called Mephistopheles, that he may come and speak with me, and dispatch again at my command, without hurt to my body, soul and goods, and diligently fulfill the will of me Thy exorcist. Fiat, fiat, fiat. Amen.

{*Thunder.*}

{*Here* FAUSTUS *may hand the book to* WAGNER *unnoticed, and so be relieved of it.*}

I conjure thee, Mephistopheles, by the unspeakable name of God, and by His virtue and power, and by Him that harrowed Hell; I conjure and exorcise thee, by angels and archangels, by thrones, dominations, principalities and powers, by virtues, by cherubim and seraphim, and by the name of thy master, Lucifer, Prince of the East, that thou do come to us, here visibly before this circle, and that thou do make answer truly, without craft or deceit, unto all my demands and questions.

{*Thunder again, and Hell-mouth opens with a great noise and a red light.*}

In the name of Him that liveth and reigneth for ever, and hath the keys of hell and of death, come hither to me, Mephistopheles.

{*Enter* MEPHISTOPHELES *out of Hell, in the form of a lion with the tail of a serpent and the feet of a bull.*}

WAGNER (looking round over FAUSTUS' shoulder)

Oh, help! help! Heaven defend us! We are lost! We're
undone. (He springs out of the circle and runs off, left. Flame and
an explosion drive him back. A peal of diabolical laughter is heard.)
Mercy! Help! what shall I do?

FAUSTUS

Spirit, I charge thee, hurt him not.

MEPHISTOPHELES

Enough. Let him go. Away with thee, mannikin! Thy
master and I have business together.
    {WAGNER runs out.}

FAUSTUS

And thou, Mephistopheles, put off this ugly shape, fit only
to frighten children. Stand before me in the semblance of
a man.

MEPHISTOPHELES

With pleasure. Nothing easier. (He takes off his lion's head and
tosses it negligently into Hell-mouth.) And now, sir, what can
I do for you, to justify the expenditure of so many big words
and this great exhibition of fi-fo-fum?

FAUSTUS

Answer me truly first concerning thyself. What art thou?

MEPHISTOPHELES

Truly, you should know best, since you called me by name.
But indeed, I am not particular. I will answer to anything
you like to call me, for my name is legion, and Evil is one
of my names.

FAUSTUS

Tell me, then, thou Evil, who made thee?

MEPHISTOPHELES

He that made all things.

FAUSTUS

What? did God make thee? Was all the evil in the world
made by God? Beware what thou sayest; I know thee for
a false and lying spirit.

MEPHISTOPHELES

That is a most unjust accusation. What lies have I ever told?
There is no need for lying, seeing that mankind are such
fools.

FAUSTUS

How so?

MEPHISTOPHELES

Why, tell them the truth and they will mislead themselves
by their own vanities and save me the trouble of invention.
I sat by Eve's shoulder in the shadow of the forbidden tree.
"Eat," said I, "and you shall become like God." She and
her silly husband ate, and it was so. Where was the lie? Was
it my fault if they persuaded themselves that God was everything they hankered to be—all-good, all-wise, all-powerful
and possessed of everlasting happiness?

FAUSTUS

Is not God all these things?

MEPHISTOPHELES

Is He these things? Look at the world He made, and ask
yourself, what is He like that made it? Would you not say it
was the work of a mad brain, cruel and blind and stupid—
this world where the thorn chokes the flower, where the fox
slays the fowl and the kite the fox, where the cat torments
the mouse for pastime before she kills it for sport? Where
men, made truly enough in the image of their Maker, rend,

ravish and torture one another, lay waste the earth, burn up provinces for a title or a handful of dirty metal, persecute for a pater-noster, and send a fellow-fool to the rack for the shape of his nose or the name of his mother's father? War, fire, famine, pestilence—is He all-good that delights in these, or all-powerful that likes them not and endures them? Ask thyself this.

FAUSTUS

I have asked it a hundred times without thy prompting. It is as though my own heart spoke to me. Man's cruelty is an abomination—but how can one justify the cruelty of God?

MEPHISTOPHELES

Is He all-wise, that had not the wits to keep out of the mess He had made, but must needs meddle with this business of being a man, and so left matters worse than He found them? Why, He could not even speak His mind plainly, but all He said was so fumblingly expressed, men have been by the ears ever since, trying to make out His meaning. And was not that a prime piece of folly, to show up His nature thus—base and ignorant as any carpenter's son, too poor in spirit to argue in His own defence, too feeble to save His own skin from the hangman? Everlasting happiness? What happiness do you find in the history of the Man of Sorrows? By their fruits ye shall know them.

FAUSTUS

It was He that said that.

MEPHISTOPHELES

So He did, in one of His more unguarded moments.

FAUSTUS

And yet, Mephistopheles, His very name has power to conjure thee from the bowels of hell.

35

MEPHISTOPHELES *(with an almost imperceptible hesitation)*

> The power is not in the name. That name is powerful only because you believe in its power. Believe in your own power, and you can command me without any tricks of conjuration.

FAUSTUS

> Wilt thou then come when I call? Wilt thou stay with me and be my servant, and do and bring me all things whatsoever I shall desire?

MEPHISTOPHELES

> I shall always be with you, John Faustus. You have only to think upon me, and I shall be there.

FAUSTUS

> And do my bidding?

MEPHISTOPHELES

> With all my power.

FAUSTUS

> Not harming me in any manner?

MEPHISTOPHELES

> You need have no more fear of me than of yourself.

FAUSTUS

> Come hither to me then, and shake hands upon the compact.

MEPHISTOPHELES

> By all means—if you will first come out of the circle.

FAUSTUS

> How can the circle hold thee back, since it has no power but by me, and I say, Come!

MEPHISTOPHELES (*again embarrassed*)

Very well argued. But the fact is, you and your servant have
so drowned the place with Jordan water that I don't care
about it. I am very susceptible to chills, and I should
infallibly get cramp in my hoofs. Besides, my Master Lucifer
forbids me to enter the circle.

FAUSTUS

And wherefore?

MEPHISTOPHELES

For the better encouragement of superstition. But come—
command me something. A few sacks of gold, perhaps, or a
little supper. You must be famished with all this nonsense
of prayer and fasting.

FAUSTUS

Well, then, bring me food.

MEPHISTOPHELES

Ho, there, my merry devils. Food and wine for your master.
Music, ho!
{*Music. Enter, right and left,* DEVILS *dancing, with platters of
fruit, etc., and one with a goblet of wine, which they present to*
FAUSTUS.}
Drink, master, drink! What! Does the cursed fruit of the tree
stick in my throat still? Drink, and drown that devil's gift of
knowledge, from whence spring all the cares that afflict
mankind. Drink—for the kingdom, the power and the glory
are within thy grasp. Only stretch out thy hand and fear not.

FAUSTUS

Spirit, I fear thee not. Give me the cup.

MEPHISTOPHELES

First sheathe that sword; my delicate devils wince
Like women to see cold iron.

37

FAUSTUS (*sheathing his sword*)

Give me the cup.
{*As* FAUSTUS *stretches his hand beyond the protection,* MEPHIS-
TOPHELES *catches him by the wrist and pulls him out of the circle.
Thunder; and all the lamps are immediately extinguished.*}
If God's so harsh a stepfather to His sons
Then must we turn adventurers, and carve out
Our own road to salvation. Here's to change! (*Drinks.*)
O the wine's brave; it dances in the blood
And whirls in the brain, glowing and giving life
As though the vintagers had put in prison
The very sun, and pressed him with the grapes
Till all the vats ran fire.

MEPHISTOPHELES (*aside*)

And so it should,
Seeing what cellars it came from.

FAUSTUS

God's old realm,
Like an estate farmed by a bankrupt, dwindles
The sluggard way to ruin; her rank hedgerows
Drop down their brambles over the sour ditch;
Bindweed, tough tares, and tangling restharrow choke
Her furrows, where the plough stands idle, rust
Reddening the share; and in her hungry fields
Only the blind mole and the skipping coney
Drive their dark tunnels 'twixt the thistle and thorn.
We'll starve at home no longer. The soul's a world,
And hath her hemispheres, as the world hath,
Where thoughts put forth like galleons, leaving behind
These weedgrown crumbling harbours shoaled with time,
To sail new seas, steer by strange stars, cross over
Unknown meridians, and by pathless coasts
Explore her dusky Indias.

MEPHISTOPHELES

Well, well, well—
I have heard young men speak thus.

38

FAUSTUS

Young men speak thus?
I am not old, Mephistopheles. I have grown
A little grey, perhaps, with study and labour,
But I'm not old at all.

MEPHISTOPHELES

Go to, go to.
{He leads FAUSTUS to the mirror.}
You are older than you should be. Mark you, mark
How lean men grow who try to save the world.
That line betwixt the brows—what wrote it there
But squinnying close at books, and frowning down
Your nose at ignorance? And the sour folds
At the corner of the mouth, the virtuous stamp
That Pharisees wear like phylacteries,
Proclaiming at what dear and grudged expense
They are chaste and sober; and the red-rimmed eyes
That weep to see how men enjoy their lusts,
Being so strangely happier than the godly.

FAUSTUS

I have wept for the woes of men, fighting like beasts,
Tortured like helpless beasts.

MEPHISTOPHELES

Let that alone,
The remedy makes it worse. Beast wars with beast
And slays and leaves no rancour. Heartbreak comes
With man's self-consciousness and righteous hate,
When one ferocious virtue meets another
As quarrelsome as itself, good savaging good
Like so many angry lobsters in a basket
Pinching each other's claws off. Now, behold
What you now are, and what you might have been
In the innocent world, if man had never meddled
With virtue and the dismal knowledge of God.
{The image of FAUSTUS fades from the mirror and the image of
the YOUNG FAUSTUS takes its place. It mimics FAUSTUS.}

FAUSTUS

Is that myself, or the young fair Apollo
Stepped from his golden chariot and new bathed
In springs of Thessaly? It moves like me
And its lips mimic mine with silent speech.
Can it be I indeed?
{*As he turns to question* MEPHISTOPHELES *the image of* HELEN
appears in the mirror behind the image of FAUSTUS *in the place
where* MEPHISTOPHELES *stands behind the real* FAUSTUS.}

MEPHISTOPHELES

Look then again.

FAUSTUS

O wonder of the world! O soul! O beauty
Beyond all splendour of stars!
{*As* FAUSTUS *moves towards the mirror,* MEPHISTOPHELES
moves to intercept him, and at the same time the image of HELEN
moves, so that as the image of FAUSTUS *clasps* HELEN, FAUSTUS
finds himself clutching MEPHISTOPHELES.}
Hence! Let me pass!
{*He breaks from* MEPHISTOPHELES. *As he touches the mirror,
the vision vanishes. Thunder again.*}
Hell and confusion! Damned, damned juggling tricks,
Nothing but sorcery!

MEPHISTOPHELES

What did you expect
When you called *me* up?

FAUSTUS

Bring her to me again
In the living flesh.

MEPHISTOPHELES

Fool, she is not for you
Nor any man. Illusion, all illusion!
For this is Grecian Helen, hell-born, hell-named,

Hell in the cities, hell in the ships, and hell
In the heart of man, seeking he knows not what.
You are too careful of your precious soul
To lay fast hold on Helen. She is mirage
Thrown on the sky by a hot reality
Far below your horizon.

FAUSTUS

          Can you not bring me
Where Helen is?

MEPHISTOPHELES

            I might—but at a cost
You might not wish to pay. In any case
Not as you are. If you would play the lover
You must look the part. Throw off this foolish weed!
Lights there!
    {*The candles are lit of their own accord.*}
            Bring forth apparel for your master,
Faustus the conjurer, Faustus the magician,
Faustus the master of the words of power,
Prince of the prince of the air!
    {*DEVILS enter and take FAUSTUS' robe and apparel him richly.*}
                 And bring him gold
To fill his purse. He must live delicately.
    {*Gold brought in a shining dish.*}
All the lost treasure of the world is ours,
That men have sweated, toiled, fought, died to gain,
And wasted—the pirate's and the gambler's spoil,
The miser's hoard, the harlot's wage, the grudged
Profits of usury, the assassin's fee,
The politician's bribe, the nation's wealth
Blown from the belching cannon—all flow down
Through veins and vessels of their native earth
In one red stream to the hot heart of hell,
Gushing and hissing—listen!
    {*Appropriate noises from Hell-mouth.*}
              The roar of the furnace!
Hark how the anvils clang in that black stithy
To the hammer-strokes forging the chains of gold

For the neck of the world, bars, ingots, cataracts
Of ringing coin! Power, power, for thy bold hand—
Take it and use it!

VOICE *(without, right)*

Alms, for the love of God,
For sweet St. Charity, pity the poor blind.
    {FAUSTUS stands arrested, with the gold in his hands.}

MEPHISTOPHELES

That is what God allows; will you allow it?

FAUSTUS

No, by the powers of Hell! If God permits
Such suffering in this damnable world, He's blind,
Deaf, mad, cruel, helpless, imbecile or dead!
    {He rushes to entrance, Mansion 1.}
Look, here is gold—gold to thy heart's desire—
No man shall want, if Faustus can prevent it.
    {He flings money out to the beggar. Cries without.}

MEPHISTOPHELES *(at Hell-mouth)*

Lucifer, Lucifer! the bird is caught—
You may turn off the lights and put the cat out,
And shut the door and go downstairs to bed.
I shall not be home for supper.
    {Laughter. Hell-mouth closes. Re-enter FAUSTUS.}
                                        These virtuous fools!

FAUSTUS

O, power is grateful to the heart—to change
Sorrow to happiness in a twinkling—blot
The word "Despair" out of life's lexicon,
And make joy blossom in the desert sand.
Bring me swift horses—bring me the wings of the wind!
We'll fly to the wide world's four distracted corners
Like a great gust of laughter, scattering delight.
We'll do—what will we not do, Mephistopheles?

42

We will forget old sins—we'll break the cross,
Tear the usurper Christ from His dark throne
And this time bury Him deep and well, beyond
All hope of resurrection.
> {Knocking at entrance, left.}
>> Hush! who's there?

WAGNER (without)

> O master, dear master, how is it with you? If you are not
> carried off body and bones into Hell, speak to me!

FAUSTUS

> All's well, Wagner. Wait. I will let thee in presently. Listen,
> Mephistopheles. You must stay with me, be known as my
> servant, show yourself only in your human shape, and not
> alarm my household too much.

MEPHISTOPHELES

> I am entirely at your service.

FAUSTUS

> Here, take my cloak. (He puts his cloak on MEPHISTOPHELES.)
> Try to look a little more respectable. You would be more
> convincing in a stout pair of boots.

MEPHISTOPHELES

> I will procure boots immediately.

FAUSTUS

> And hark'ee. See that you offer no offense to Lieschen. She
> is a good, modest, virtuous child.

MEPHISTOPHELES

> Set your mind at rest. On such as her I have no power.

FAUSTUS

And be gentle with my poor Wagner. So. I will open the
door. (Crossing left, he turns and adds a fierce whisper.) Tuck
your tail up! (At entrance.) Come in, Wagner.
{Enter WAGNER.}

WAGNER

O Doctor, Doctor, praise God you're safe and sound. Lisa
and I have been so frightened. Such dreadful noises—and
the thunder—the whole house shook. We've been saying our
prayers in the kitchen. Do forgive me for being so foolish and
cowardly. I thought you were killed and the devil had eaten
you, so I came to see if I could do anything. Has the devil
gone away? The rooms smells shockingly of sulphur.

FAUSTUS

There's nobody here but this—gentleman, whom I have
engaged to be my personal attendant.

WAGNER (to MEPHISTOPHELES)

How do you do, sir? God be with you. (Calling off.) It's all
right, Lisa. The devil's gone. (To MEPHISTOPHELES.) What
a dreadful night to arrive in. Are you wet? Perhaps you
would like to change your shoes? I could lend you slippers.
It's so unwise to sit in damp feet. What size do you . . . ?
Oh, I beg your pardon (to FAUSTUS). How thoughtless of
me. I didn't notice the poor creature was so afflicted.

FAUSTUS

You are too officious.

MEPHISTOPHELES (to WAGNER)

It's very kind of you, but I came—by the underground way.

WAGNER

I see. Well (anxious to do something), the room is very untidy.
Shall I help you off with your robe, Doctor? Dear me, it's
off already. What a fine suit of clothes you have got!

44

VOICES (without)

> Help! Help! . . . Hand over the money! . . . Thieves!
> Murder! . . . Strike him down . . . Give me the gold . . .
> Ah! would you! . . . Down with you! (Noise of fighting.)

LISA (off)

> Help, watchman, help! Watch! Watch!

FAUSTUS

> What is all that?

MEPHISTOPHELES

> The effects of your benevolence, I fancy.
> {Enter LISA, left.}

LISA

> Alas! alas! Here's a poor old blind man been set upon and
> robbed under our windows and a whole crowd of ruffians
> quarrelling for the money. I saw three men stabbed. (Noise
> increases.) Oh, mercy.

FAUSTUS

> Are men mad to abuse the gifts we give them? (He rushes off,
> Mansion 1, drawing his sword as he goes.) What is God about?

WAGNER

> I don't understand all this.

MEPHISTOPHELES (primly)

> Indiscriminate charity is a device of the devil.

LISA (with a little shriek)

> Oh, Wagner, who's that?

MEPHISTOPHELES

> The Doctor's servant, so please you.

LISA (recoiling against WAGNER)

I don't like him. I'm afraid of him. Who is he?

WAGNER

Bless me, Lisa, where are your manners? (LISA drops
MEPHISTOPHELES *a reluctant curtsey and escapes, left.*) You
must excuse her. We have all been upset by the thunder-
storm. *(With holy-water stoup.)* Oh, dear, this is empty again.
(He hands it to MEPHISTOPHELES.) Do you mind holding it
while I fill it up?
      {*Goes up to shelf, back.*}

MEPHISTOPHELES

Pray don't apologise. Women have their fancies. I get along
very well with them as a rule, but every so often, the nicest
girls will take a positive dislike to me. I've no idea why.

WAGNER (returning with flask)

Very strange—but as you say, girls are quite unaccountable.
Please hold it carefully. This is very special Holy Water
from the——
      {*Re-enter FAUSTUS, Mansion 1.*}

FAUSTUS

The watch have arrested them all—Wagner! leave that
alone!
      {*He is too late. The water steams up and bubbles over the bowl,
      which MEPHISTOPHELES lets fall.*}

WAGNER (crossing himself)

Holy Mary! Heaven deliver us! Oh, sir, sir; I fear me you
are gotten into very ill company.

MEPHISTOPHELES

So that cat's out of the bag!

FAUSTUS

What will you do, Wagner? Will you quit my service?

WAGNER

No, Doctor, no. I'll not leave you alone to face danger
again. I'm sorry for what I did. But from henceforth I'll be
as brave as a lion.

FAUSTUS

Thanks, my faithful Wagner.

MEPHISTOPHELES *(clapping WAGNER on the back)*

Why, that's a bold fellow, to be ready to live cheek by jowl
with the devil.

WAGNER

Why, so must every Christian man. And the devil we see is
less terrible than the devil we don't see *(shaking MEPHIS-
TOPHELES off)*. But there's no need to be familiar. *(To
FAUSTUS)* And what happens next, if you please?

FAUSTUS

We're off to Rome, to beard God in His own stronghold.

WAGNER *(stolidly)*

Are you going by sea, or—underground?

MEPHISTOPHELES

Through the air, my lad. By enchantment.

FAUSTUS

Those winged dragons you are always talking about.

WAGNER *(drily)*

Just as well. You were always a very poor sailor.

FAUSTUS

You and Lisa can do as you like. Come, Mephistopheles!
{*He goes out, right.*}

WAGNER (*going off, left*)

Poor Lisa! She won't like this very much. (*Turning suddenly.*)
Here, you! Clear up all this mess. And look sharp. I'm
going to pack.
{*Exit.*}

MEPHISTOPHELES (*staring after him*)

Well, I'll be—blessed!
{*He claps his hands. Music, and enter four DEVILS, who clear the
stage. MEPHISTOPHELES goes out by the same way as FAUSTUS.*}

SCENE II (Mansion 3)

Rome—The Forum

{Enter from Mansion 1 (Wittenberg) WAGNER and LISA in travelling dress, with luggage. They walk all about the stage and come at last to Rome (Mansion 3).}

WAGNER

Here we are at last—safely in Rome! It has been a long journey from Wittenberg.

LISA

Long and wearisome! I'm so grateful to you, kind Wagner, for coming with me, instead of flying away on the winged dragon with Dr. Faustus and—that other, terrible man.

WAGNER

I shouldn't dream of letting you travel unprotected. Besides, I have thought it all over and decided that winged dragons are all right for learned philosophers, but plain folk like you and me do best on the beaten track. (Looking about him.) What a fine city Rome is, to be sure! A hundred times bigger than Wittenberg.

LISA

How shall we ever find the Doctor out, in this great labyrinth of streets and houses?

WAGNER

We shall find him, never fear. During all these months he will certainly have become very great and famous. This wide square must be the market-place. Let's sit down here

49

and rest, and presently we will ask some passer-by to direct us to the Doctor's lodging.

{*They sit down, left. Enter, from Mansion 3, a CARDINAL and a PRIEST conversing; they come down centre.*}

CARDINAL

If such be the case, then His Holiness should be told about it. And in the meantime, by all means speak to the people.

PRIEST

I assure Your Eminence, it is as I say. The whole city is disturbed by the miracles of Dr. Faustus.

WAGNER (*to* LISA)

There! what did I tell you?

CARDINAL

Where does he come from?

PRIEST

From Wittenberg, they say, some twelve months since. His learning is undoubtedly great and his wealth unlimited; though how he came by them, God or the devil knows. He distributes told to all and sundry, heals the sick, raises the dead, and corrupts the minds of the poor by his vile, atheistical talk. The churches are deserted. Sundays and week-days, the people throng to the lectures of Dr. Faustus.

LISA (*approaching them*)

O Father! If you know Dr. Faustus, pray tell me where he is to be found.

PRIEST

What! Is this another of them? Away, shameless girl.

CARDINAL

The less you have to do with John Faustus the better. His life is scandalous, his followers godless—

PRIEST

Heretical—

CARDINAL

Idolaters—

PRIEST

Sorcerers—

CARDINAL

Whoremongers—

PRIEST

Devil-worshippers—

CARDINAL

Apostate—

PRIEST

Excommunicate—

CARDINAL

And irretrievably damned!

LISA

No, no! if you knew him you would not say such things. He is good and kind.

WAGNER

The most learned man in Christendom.

PRIEST

He is the open enemy of God and Holy Church.

CARDINAL

And known to be in league with the devil. (As WAGNER
winces at this home-thrust.) Will you deny it?

LISA

Alas!

WAGNER (stoutly)

If Dr. Faustus commands the spirits it is to a good and pious
end. He is very clever, and knows how to bind the devil to
the service of God.

CARDINAL

You are sadly deceived. It is forbidden to cast out devils by
Beelzebub. Nor will a good end justify such vile and wicked
means.

WAGNER (drawing LISA away)

Come away, Lisa. They are jealous of him. We will ask
somebody else.

PRIEST (pulling CARDINAL across, right)

Besides, Eminence, the end he seeks is very dangerous.
    {Various TOWNSFOLK begin to drift in, Mansion 3 and left.
    MEPHISTOPHELES enters and stands, right, showing in pantomime
    that he overhears the conversation of CARDINAL and PRIEST.}
He preaches everywhere that he can abolish pain and suffering from the world. And what, pray, would become of
religion, if there were no such thing as suffering?

CARDINAL

What, indeed? Who would repent of sin, if he did not fear to
suffer in this world. Or if pain and sickness were not there,
to put him in mind of his latter end?

PRIEST

Nobody would go to confession, or pay for masses, or indul-
gences, or prayers for the sick. There would be no pilgrim-
ages, no alms-giving, no thank-offerings, no rich bequests to
the Church. And what would happen to us, I should like to
know? No sin, no sermon; no cross, no cardinal; no pain, no
Pope!
{MEPHISTOPHELES *withdraws again.*}

CARDINAL

Quite so; but I should not stress that point in your address.
Begin now. I will go and acquaint His Holiness with all this.
{PRIEST *mounts the rostrum, left.*}
Give ear, good people. The reverened father has somewhat to
say to you.
{*Exit* CARDINAL, *Mansion 3.* FAUSTUS *and* MEPHISTOPHELES
enter unnoticed at back of CROWD, *who gather right.*}

PRIEST

Citizens of Rome! Sons and daughters of Holy Church! It
has come to the ears of His Holiness the Pope that many
among you are led away by the abominable doctrines of one
John Faustus—(*cheers for* FAUSTUS)—a charlatan, a sorcerer,
a man of lewd and evil life (*cries of dissent*) who would delude
you by the promise to do away with toil and labour, with
poverty, pain and suffering, and ensure to every man health,
wealth and long days upon the earth. (*Renewed cheers.*) Alas,
my children, why will you be deceived? Do you not know
that toil and suffering were ordained by God for the sins of
Adam? And that only by suffering are you made worthy to
enter into the joys of Heaven? Do you think there is any way
to salvation, except by the cross whereon our Saviour
suffered for the sins of all? (*Murmurs of doubt.*) All of you will
come to die some day—and how will you answer then for a
life spent in sloth and luxury? Will it be easy, think you, to
put off that proud and stubborn flesh that no suffering has
mortified, no sorrow subdued? Let not the lust of gold corrupt you, for it is easier for a camel to pass through the eye
of a needle than for a rich man to enter into the Kingdom of

Heaven. Turn away your hearts from idols; embrace the
cross and repent; return to the bosom of Holy Church, to
whom alone it is given to bind and loose and free you from
the domination of evil. If this fellow Faustus seeks to persuade you from your allegiance to the Church, it is that he
may destroy your souls. He is a damned soul, burning in a
hell of hatred, and would drag you all down along with him
to damnation.

FAUSTUS *(leaping upon the rostrum, right)*

That is a lie!

PRIEST

Who dares to say so?

FAUSTUS

I say so. I am John Faustus.

PRIEST

Silence, thou rascal!

FAUSTUS

I will not be silent. I tell you to your face that your Church
is corrupt, your doctrine a lie and your God a cruel tyrant.
{*Murmurs among the crowd.* MEPHISTOPHELES *whispers in*
FAUSTUS' *ear.*}

PRIEST

Out of thine own mouth, athiest! Do you hear this fellow
blaspheme against God and His Holy Church?

FAUSTUS

The Church? Hark to the sly priest with his own axe to
grind! The Church is rich and you are poor. Her prelates go
in rich robes, and you in stinking rags. Wherefore? Ask him
that preaches the money out of your pockets to keep him
and his greasy brethren in idleness. He cares nothing for
your souls, but only for the gold he can squeeze out of you.

PRIEST

It is false.

FAUSTUS

It is true. Ask my servant here, that heard him say as
much to the Cardinal.

CROWD

Shame! shame! . . . Down with the idle priests!

FAUSTUS

Why should you slave to enrich these blood-suckers?

CROWD (rushing towards PRIEST)

Blood-suckers! . . . Horse-leeches! . . . Down with the priests!
. . . Sack the monasteries! . . . Come on! . . . Sack! slay! . . .
Away with them! etc.

PRIEST

Beware! Touch not God's annointed!
    {CROWD hesitates.}
Think, before you call down the terrible vengeance of
Heaven. What saith the Scripture? Thou shalt not suffer a
witch to live. Faustus is a witch and a sorcerer, and his
servant is the devil incarnate. By their fruits ye shall know
them. They work the works of darkness, and their gifts shall
bring, not blessings, but a curse. Is that no so?

FIRST WOMAN

It is so. We were poor, and Faustus gave us gold. Now my
husband has left his home and gone to live wantonly with
harlots.

FIRST MAN

I was a cripple and lived by begging. Faustus cured me, and
now I must work to live.

55

SECOND WOMAN

I was barren, and Faustus laid his spells upon me, and now I have borne a child that is possessed by seven devils.

SECOND MAN

I loved my wife, and she died. Faustus raised her from the dead and lo! she is become a shrew, a vixen, the veriest termagant in Rome.

WIFE

Thou are a beast to say so. Take that, coward!
{She beats her husband. Laughter and commotion.}

FAUSTUS

Ungrateful dogs!—

PRIEST

Hark, how he turns upon you now!

CROWD

Down with him! . . . Sorcerer! . . . Witch! . . . Burn him! . . . Drown him! . . . Tear him to pieces! . . . Witch! Witch! Witch!
{A rush is made against FAUSTUS.}

FAUSTUS (in a tone of command)

Mephistopheles!

MEPHISTOPHELES

Back, little men! (The CROWD is frozen into immobility.) You cannot move hand or foot to harm my master.

CROWD

What's this? . . . I am paralysed . . . I am turned to stone . . . I can't lift my arm . . . I can't put my foot down . . . etc.

MEPHISTOPHELES

A nice lot of fools you look! A most edifying regiment of
wax-works! And Master Priest there, fixed on one foot, like
an image of Hermes in a garden-pool! Pray, sir, are you
afflicted with a sudden cramp? Why not take counsel of Dr.
Faustus, that is so eminent a physician? Shall I tickle them
for you, master? Shall I twist their bones? Shall I put fire under
their tails?

FAUSTUS

Enough! release them, Mephistopheles.
　　{The CROWD put down their arms and legs again and stand
　　rubbing themselves foolishly.}
O men, men! Why will you quarrel and fight? Why seek to
harm me, that have only loved you and laboured for your
good? I would free you from the burden of fear and pain and
poverty that God has laid upon you. Listen to me. If God
made all things, He made the evil that torments you, and
why should you serve so cruel a master? If He made not all
things, He is not God, and you may defy Him as I do. Be
men! Rouse yourselves! Throw off this bondage of superstition, and learn to know your friends from your foes. I am
not your enemy. God is the enemy of us all——
　　{Enter, Mansion 3, the POPE, carrying a crucifix in his hand,
　　and with CARDINAL in attendance.}

POPE

Then learn to face the enemy. Speak on, my child.
I stand here for God.

CROWD (falling to their knees)

　　　　　　The Holy Father!

FAUSTUS

Stand, then, old man, and hear what I would spit
Into God's teeth, were we set face to face
Even in the Courts of Heaven. God's heart is evil,
Vengeful and tyrannous. He hates the flesh,

The sweet flesh that He made; He treads down beauty
In the winepress of His wrath, pashing it out
To the sour wine of sacrifice; His eye
Is jaundiced to behold such happiness
As men may snatch out of a tortured world.
Look on the symbol in thy hand—the sceptre
Thou rul'st with in His name—it is the yardstick,
The very measure of the devilish hatred
He bears to man, were man His very Son.
Men! I stand here for man, and in man's name
{*He springs upon the Pope and snatches the cruciflx from him.*}
Defy God's rule, break His accursed sceptre
And smite His regent down.
{*He lifts the crucifix to slay the POPE. the CROWD exhibit horror,
but are held back by MEPHISTOPHELES.*}

WAGNER (*throwing himself between them*)

O master, master!

FAUSTUS (*flinging WAGNER off*)

You here? Stand aside!

LISA (*catching FAUSTUS by the arm*)

Oh, Doctor, dear Doctor! for shame! What! Strike an old man—
helpless—unresisting?
{*FAUSTUS pauses in some confusion.*}
Oh, no! how could you dream of it? You will not. I know
you will not. Not the devil himself could change your kind
heart so. And you will not break the image of our dear
Lord, who loved us so well and gave His life for us!
{*During this speech, MEPHISTOPHELES retreats and the CROWD
closes threateningly in on FAUSTUS.*}

FAUSTUS (*letting the crucifix drop into WAGNER'S hands*)

O Lisa, Lisa!
{*He looks about him, sees the menacing looks of the CROWD and
goes on in an exhausted voice:*}
I too love men; but they are all against me.
They hug their chains; the sacrificial iron

58

Cankers them at the core. I am not afraid
To suffer; for their sakes I would be damned
Willingly, so I first might do away
Suffering for ever from the pleasant earth.
And here stands power, like a smooth engine, ready
For good or ill alike. Being powerful,
I might be happy—might I not be happy?—
But still the cry of the poor is in my ears
Intolerably. *(To the* POPE): You they call Holy Father—
A kind, compassionate title, "Holy Father"—
Will you be blind to truth? God, having power,
Uses it like a devil; if He were good
He would turn back the ruthless wheel of time
To the golden age again. I am not God,
But can command the devil's power to serve
Good ends. Which is the devil—God, or I?
Do you be judge between us.

POPE

                   O my poor child,
How much unhappiness is in store for thee!
For thou art taken in the toils of God,
That are more delicate than the spider's thread,
More strong than iron; and though thou wander far
As hell from Heaven, His cunning hand shall twitch
The line, and draw thee home. There is no rest
For such as thee, that bear upon their hearts
The brand of God, and, warring against God,
Make war upon themselves. Thou must be patient,
For God is very patient. Dost thou think
I cannot feel thy griefs? I am the Pope,
Set on a tower above the plains of time
To watch how evil is at odds with good,
And to abide the issue, helpless, save
As prayer and wisdom and the grace of God
Shall give me strength. Hard it is, very hard,
To travel up the slow and stony road
To Calvary, to redeem mankind; far better
To make but one resplendent miracle,
Lean through the cloud, lift the right hand of power
And with a sudden lightning smite the world perfect.

59

Yet this was not God's way, Who had the power,
But set it by, choosing the cross, the thorn,
The sorrowful wounds. Something there is, perhaps,
That power destroys in passing, something supreme,
To whose great value in the eyes of God
That cross, that thorn, and those five wounds bear witness.
Son, go in peace; for thou hast sinned through love;
To such sin God is merciful. Not yet
Has thy familiar devil persuaded thee
To that last sin against the Holy Ghost
Which is, to call good evil, evil good.
Only for that is no forgiveness—Not
That God would not forgive all sins there are,
Being what He is; but that this sin destroys
The power to feel His pardon, so that damnation
Is consequence, not vengeance; and indeed
So all damnation is. I will pray for thee.
And you, my children, go home, gird your loins
And light your lamps, beseeching God to bring
His kingdom nearer, in what way He will.
{*Exeunt* POPE, CARDINAL *and* PRIEST, *Mansion 3.* CROWD
go out left and right. Manent FAUSTUS, LISA, WAGNER *and*
MEPHISTOPHELES.}

MEPHISTOPHELES (*somersaulting across the stage and bowing
derisively after the retreating* POPE)

Go in peace, old gentleman, go in peace! Did ever a man
use so many words to confess his own incompetence? That
fellow has no business in Peter's seat—he ought to be in
in Parliament. Come, Master—will you take the road to
Calvary, and sup at the Skull-and-Crossbones?

FAUSTUS

I am tired, tired, Mephistopheles. Follow Christ? That way
is too long and too uncertain.

MEPHISTOPHELES

His way was folly and failure. I told you so, and now the
Pope confirms it. Take your own way, in the devil's name,
and shake a little sense into mankind.

60

FAUSTUS

My way frightens them. They have not even the heart to
be grateful for my gifts.

WAGNER (simply)

Well, they are the devil's gifts after all. Perhaps it's true that
they don't turn out very well. I'm sure people were very
grateful in Wittenberg. Don't you remember? All those
presents of fish and vegetables? I had hard work to carry
them home.

LISA

Won't you come back to Wittenberg and heal the sick with
your drugs and simples as you did before? Indeed, indeed
you were happier then.

FAUSTUS

Much happier, Lisa.

MEPHISTOPHELES

If you were happy, why did you send for me?

WAGNER (threatening MEPHISTOPHELES with the crucifix)

Will you kindly go away and stop interfering?
    {MEPHISTOPHELES retreats.}

LISA

They are waiting for you, Doctor, and longing for your
return—all the poor and the sorrowful, and the mothers
with their sick children. They love you so much—we all love
you in Wittenberg.

FAUSTUS

Do they love me, Lisa? Do you think that is happiness, after
all? To take the easy way—to love and be beloved, and not
trouble to understand or get things altered? Perhaps. Every
day the same sun rises, and year by year the spring returns.

Have the swallows built again under the eaves of my window?

LISA

Oh, yes! Before we left home there were five speckled eggs in the nest.

FAUSTUS

There is peace in those quiet streets, cool and deep beneath the leaning gables. Let us go home, and find a little love before we die. They love me in Wittenberg. . . . Do you love me, Lisa?

LISA

Alas! I think I have loved you all my life.

WAGNER

Oh, God!

MEPHISTOPHELES

Didn't you know that? Any fool could have seen it.

FAUSTUS

Poor child! You should find a better lover. I am growing old, Lisa. I have forgotten how to love.

WAGNER

I am a fool indeed. But that's nothing new.

LISA

You are the most wonderful man in all the world—far too great and good for me.

FAUSTUS

Hush! that is foolishness. But a very sweet foolishness. Look at me. Your eyes are like quiet pools with the stars reflected in them.

MEPHISTOPHELES

Cheer up, fool. I know how to deal with this.

WAGNER

I don't want any of your help.

MEPHISTOPHELES

But *she* does. Do you think he cares twopence for her?

FAUSTUS

My head aches. I am homesick. Take me in your arms and comfort me.

LISA

With all my heart.

MEPHISTOPHELES

Hush-a-bye, baby, on the tree-top! Do you call this love?

WAGNER

What else do you call it?

MEPHISTOPHELES

Childishness. All men are fretful children when they can't get their own way. Love? Fiddlesticks!

LISA

Does it ache much?

FAUSTUS

Not now. There is rest in your presence, because there is rest in your soul.

MEPHISTOPHELES

Rest, indeed? We'll see about that. Sacripant! Belphegor!
{*Calling off.*}

FAUSTUS

What was that song you used to sing while the bread was
a-baking? All about Kings and Queens?

LISA

That little, nursery song?

MEPHISTOPHELES (calling off)

Here's a soul drowsing into Paradise. Whips! Whips!

LISA (sings)

Five silver fishes swimming in the sea,
Five gold birds in a sycamore tree,
{Enter HELEN, right, with DEVILS attending her.}
Five red deer running over the land,
Five jewel-rings upon my hand.

MEPHISTOPHELES (in the ear of FAUSTUS)

Master, where are your eyes?

FAUSTUS

Gadfly! Let me sleep.

LISA (sings)

When trees grow tall and leaves grow green
You shall be king and I shall be queen.

MEPHISTOPHELES

Nay, dream on if you will. Sloth is a sin and serves my purpose; though there are merrier ways to be damned.

FAUSTUS (freeing his eyes from LISA'S hand and sitting up)

Away with you to hell. Be off, I say. (He sees HELEN.) O my
soul!

HELEN

    John Faustus!

FAUSTUS (leaping to his feet)

    Call me across a void of empty stars
    And I shall hear.

HELEN

              O love, hast thou forgotten?

FAUSTUS

    Not till the seas run dry; not till the centre
    Kiss the circumference, and time's iron hand
    Crack the great axle of the world asunder!
    O Helen, Helen, Helen, I have loved thee
    Before time was.

LISA

            Come back, sweet love, come back!

WAGNER

    Master, beware! 'Tis witchcraft.

FAUSTUS

                    It is the voice
    Of all the world's desire.

LISA

               Oh, he is lost.
    {She falls into the arms of WAGNER, who helps her off.}

FAUSTUS

    In what miraculous dream, in what far land,
    Under what magic boughs, did thou and I
    Lie once, and watch the sun shift through the leaves
    Glinting the golden apples, when Troy town

Was yet unbuilt, that now is but a song
Almost beyond all memory? When did we learn
Immortal love? What unimagined page
Of scripture holds our legendary names,
Faustus and Helen?

HELEN

                    My name is Helen now;
God's wrath, and ruin of distressful stars
Have made me so accurst. But once, ah, once
Adam lay on my breast and called me Lilith—
Long, long ago, in the old, innocent garden
Before Eve came, bringing her gift of knowledge
And shame where no shame was. The sons of Eve
Are all ashamed of me.

FAUSTUS

                    Are all athirst
For thee, thou star of more than mortal hope
To men!

HELEN

          Shame and desire eat out their hearts,
For they are Adam's seed. And thou wast Adam,
Whose boyhood love was mine. So, when I call,
Thou canst not choose but turn to me again
From the very arms of Eve. Bone of thy bone
Is she, earth of the earth; she gives thee rest,
As the kind earth shall rest thy bones at last.
I am the fire in the heart, the plague eternal
Of vain regret for joys that are no more.

FAUSTUS

Wherefore no more? I have returned to thee
Across the barren ways of world and time;
My soul is in thy breast. Take me to thee,
That we may love and laugh in innocence
With the everlasting gods! Devils, stand back!
I will to Helen. In the tremendous name

Of power ineffable, by the seven-fold seal
Of Adonai, back!
{*The* DEVILS *restrain him still.*}
What barrier's here
My witchcraft cannot break?

HELEN

The bitter knowledge
Of good and evil. None may touch my lips
While on his own hangs still the fatal taste
Of Eve's sharp apple.

FAUSTUS

Paris had thy kiss.

HELEN

Paris cast back the apple to the gods,
Whose ringing discord jarred the towers of Troy
In ruin down.

FAUSTUS

And so will I; let ruin
Roar like a cataract and drown the world!
Knowledge, begone! All part and lot in Eve
I here renounce. Thou, Mephistopheles,
Serpent of Eden, take thy curse again,
Undo the sin of Adam, turn the years
Back to their primal innocence. By thine oath
Sworn in the mouth of hell, and by the power
Of all my magical art, I do command thee!

MEPHISTOPHELES

Softly, softly. What a hurry you are in! You impetuous
young lovers want everything done in a moment. Take
away the knowledge of good and evil? That's rather an
unusual order.

FAUSTUS

Can it be done, or no?

MEPHISTOPHELES

Oh, it can be *done*. Everything can be *done*. But we have to charge a price for that sort of thing.

FAUSTUS

Quick. Name it. What price?

MEPHISTOPHELES

The usual price. Your soul.

FAUSTUS

Take it. Sin and soul together.

MEPHISTOPHELES

And we can't sell you eternal youth upon freehold. I could manage a twenty-four years' lease if that would suit you.

FAUSTUS

It would be worth it, were it twenty-four hours or twenty-four minutes.

MEPHISTOPHELES

Very well. It's a bargain. *(Calling off towards Hell-mouth.)* Ho, there! Bring me the bond.
    {HELEN *vanishes, the stage darkens.*}
Drawn in the name of John Faustus and of me, Mephistopheles. He to abjure and renounce the worship and service of God, and to enjoy in exchange eternal youth and primal innocence for four-and-twenty years; at the end of which term he, the said John Faustus, shall become forfeit to the Devil, and be carried away, soul and spirit, body and bones, to Hell.

FAUSTUS

Quickly! Where is Helen gone? The air grows thick. My
senses swim. The walls of Rome swoon into darkness about
me.

MEPHISTOPHELES

Walls of Rome? Nonsense! You are in your own study at
Wittenberg. See! There are the lit candles (the candles on the
walls are lit). And your magic mirror (the mirror becomes
luminous). And your servants about you.
    {WAGNER and LISA creep in to stand beside FAUSTUS.}

FAUSTUS

Where is the bond? I will sign it with my blood.

WAGNER

Master, think again.

LISA

For thy dear soul's sake, take Christ's way, not this way.
    {The image of HELEN is seen in the mirror.}

FAUSTUS

I come, I come, sweet Helen. Mephistopheles! The bond!
Make haste.
    {Hell-mouth opens. Enter a DEVIL with the bond.}

MEPHISTOPHELES

It is here.

FAUSTUS

A pen—give me a pen. Where is the table?

MEPHISTOPHELES

Here.
    {Two DEVILS enter, bearing a board, which they offer to
    FAUSTUS, kneeling, as though for a table.}

Pluck forth thy dagger. Prick thine arm. Write.
{FAUSTUS *pricks his arm.* MEPHISTOPHELES *puts the pen into his hand.*}

FAUSTUS

See how the red stream runs upon the table like letters written in fire. *Homo, fuge*—Flee, O man. What, shall I turn back now? *(Thunder.)* A dreadful voice cries in my ear: Flee from the wrath to come! O, whither shall I fly?

LISA

Fly to the arms of God.

FAUSTUS

To the arms of love. Sweet Helen, receive my soul. *(He signs the bond. Thunder again.)* So, it is done.

MEPHISTOPHELES

Done! And so clap hands on the bargain. *(Diabolic laughter.* MEPHISTOPHELES *tosses the bond to the* DEVIL, *who returns with it to Hell. Hell-mouth shuts.)* Come now, go to thy Helen as a new-made man.

FAUSTUS

How now? What wilt thou do to me?

MEPHISTOPHELES *(leading him to the mirror, where the image of the* YOUNG FAUSTUS *now appears beside* HELEN)

Have courage, my master, my bold conjurer, my masterful great magician. See, it's as simple as walking through a mirror. In with you, in with you!
{MEPHISTOPHELES *pushes* FAUSTUS *before him into the mirror, and* HELEN *and the* YOUNG FAUSTUS *walk out of it.*}

FAUSTUS

Oh, I am free!

YOUNG FAUSTUS

I am free! Come, Helen, to my arms!
{*As* YOUNG FAUSTUS *embraces* HELEN *and carries her off, right,*
MEPHISTOPHELES *carries away the old body of* FAUSTUS *behind
the mirror, which grows dark.*}

LISA

He has fled from us into a dream. He has left the world
empty. I am afraid of this thing that looks with his eyes and
speaks with his voice.

WAGNER

It is Faustus and not Faustus. A stranger—yet I feel as
though I had known him a long time.

LISA

It is the shadow of an imagination. . . . How still the town
is! No stir of wheel or footfall; no chime of the clock; no
watchman's voice.

WAGNER

And how dark! but not with the darkness of night. It is like
the dusk and silence that creep before an eclipse.

LISA

My sun is eclipsed for ever.

WAGNER

Poor Lisa! I know by my own heart how sorrowful you
must be.

LISA

And I know by mine how bitterly I have hurt you. Forgive
me, Chrostopher. We cannot help ourselves.

WAGNER

Please don't trouble about me. It really isn't worth it. It was
presumptuous of me to set my hopes so high. One must
expect disappointment in this world. *(Stoutly.)* And you
know I am very absent-minded. I shall quite often forget to
be miserable.

LISA

Dear, good Christopher. What a comfort you are! . . . I'm
sorry. I feel so desolate. I can't help crying.

WAGNER

There, there!
*{He puts his arm round her and pats her shoulder consolingly.
MEPHISTOPHELES slithers in and speaks in his ear.}*

MEPHISTOPHELES

Christopher, Christopher! Shall I bring her to your bed?

WAGNER *(whisking round)*

What the devil? . . .
*{LISA sees MEPHISTOPHELES and springs away with a faint
shriek.}*
So it's you again!

MEPHISTOPHELES

Clever lad! Now's your chance. Say the word, and I'll
tumble her into your arms like a ripe plum.

WAGNER

Don't be disgusting.

MEPHISTOPHELES

Oh, but you want her, Christopher.

WAGNER

No, I don't. Not if she doesn't want me. You needn't think she'd listen to you. Anything *you* brought me wouldn't be Lisa at all, but something nasty in her shape. I know your tricks by heart. They're all in the conjuring book.

LISA

What's he saying, Christopher?

WAGNER

A lot of filthy nonsense. Don't mind him.

LISA

I've been thinking what to do. Since our dear master is out of his mind, we must stay close to him and perhaps find some way to restore him.

WAGNER

To be sure we will.

LISA

And we will try and to do his work—help the poor and heal the sick with the remedies he taught us. And when God sees what we are doing, He will say: "That is the real Faustus; that's what he really meant to do. Faustus is still doing good by his servants' hands."

WAGNER

I always said you were clever. I should never have thought of that.

LISA

So you see, our work will plead for our master's soul.

WAGNER

Of course it will.

MEPHISTOPHELES

You flatter yourselves. I can't understand how men can be such fools.

WAGNER

Very likely not. There's a great deal you can't understand, you nasty, ignorant, dirty-minded demon. So hold your tongue and be damned to you!

MEPHISTOPHELES (going)

That is a very superfluous wish. Good evening.

WAGNER

Hi! Stop! What have you done with Dr. Faustus?

MEPHISTOPHELES (airily)

We are just starting on a grand tour of the world. The Duchess Helen accompanies us. You might call it a little honeymoon trip. Constantinople. The Pyramids. Morocco. Persia. The Caucasus. The Earthly Paradise. All carried out in first-class style; a chariot-de-luxe with six dragons——

WAGNER

You don't say so. Then you can saddle me a chimaera—two chimaeras; and see that one of them is trained to carry a lady.

MEPHISTOPHELES

Certainly, certainly. Shall I charge them to your account, or the Doctor's?

WAGNER (firmly)

You will include transport and service under your all-in terms. Did you bring our baggage from Rome?

MEPHISTOPHELES

I'm afraid it was overlooked in the hurry.

WAGNER

Then fetch it. At once. Do you hear, you lazy devil?

MEPHISTOPHELES

Immediately.
{WAGNER's and LISA's baggage is wafted in from the direction
of Rome. Noise of wheels and trampling, off, right.}
Excuse me, the chariot is at the door.
{MEPHISTOPHELES hurries off, Mansion 1.}

WAGNER

Come, Lisa. Dry your eyes. Be brave. Needs must when the
devil drives. (Cracking of whips, with snorting and trampling, off,
right.) There's no time to waste in virtuous foot-slogging.
Come Heaven, come Hell, we'll follow our Master Faustus.
{Exeunt WAGNER and LISA, Mansion 1.}

FAUSTUS (off, right)

Stand back, there. Give them their heads.

WAGNER (off, right)

Up with you, Lisa. My stirrup, Mephistopheles.

MEPHISTOPHELES (off, right)

To the four winds—away!
{The infernal cavalcade is heard to rise in the air and fly off.}

SCENE III (Mansion 2)

Innsbrück—The Emperor's Court

{*Enter from Heaven, the Angel AZRAEL. He turns, as though answering someone inside.*}

AZRAEL

Yes, sir. Certainly, sir. No difficulty at all, sir. Everything is quite in order.
{*He comes down and on, left, and walks briskly across to Mansion 2, sorting a sheaf of papers as he goes. At the entrance to the Mansion, he bumps, in a preoccupied way, into MEPHISTOPHELES coming out, and apologises without looking at him.*}
Sorry; my fault.
{*Exit into Mansion.*}

MEPHISTOPHELES (*looking after him*)

Stuck-up snob! Can't even recognise an old companion
who's come down in the world. (*Coming down-stage; in the
voice of an impatient man summoning a waiter.*) Demons! demons!
. . . the service is getting very slack. . . . Oh, for Satan's sake,
hurry up there!
{*Enter a DEVIL, right.*}
The fool wants another job done. A trifle for the Empress.
Flowers out of season with ripe fruit and blossom on the
same branch. Fetch it and look sharp. . . . Where from?
How the devil should I know? Try the Hesperides. (*Exit
DEVIL, left; MEPHISTOPHELES sits down and registers fatigue.*)
This is the worst term of hard labour I ever undertook. If
my four-and-twenty years were not up to-night, I should go
on strike.
{*Re-enter, Mansion 2, AZRAEL, with a baby in his arms.*}
Good morning, my lord Azrael.

AZRAEL

Why, it's Mephistopheles! Good morning. And how's the world with you? You're looking a little exhausted.

MEPHISTOPHELES

Yes, I dare say. What's that you've got there? Contraband?

AZRAEL

No, no. Nobody you've any claim on. A sweet and pious soul, born anew as a little child into the Kingdom of our Father. Do you want to see her papers? (MEPHISTOPHELES *extends his hand in grim silence.*) Suspicious old devil, aren't you?

MEPHISTOPHELES *(examining papers)*

So that's who it is.

AZRAEL

One of your failures, Mephistopheles. Nothing for you there at all. Not so much as a whiff of Purgatory fire. Only a brief educational course in the heavenly kindergarten. Satisfied?

MEPHISTOPHELES *(returning papers with a grunt)*

All right. Just as well. We're run off our hoofs already. My client Faustus——

AZRAEL

Yes. You've been keeping our department pretty busy too. We were working overtime to deal with all those poor souls parted from their bodies at the battle of Pavia. That was your show, wasn't it?

MEPHISTOPHELES

And a damned good show, too. I had fifteen legions of devils fighting on the Emperor's side, to say nothing of a magical tempest and a great quantity of heavy artillery forged in our own works. To-day, we propose to sack Rome, with lavish accompaniments of loot, rape, and carnage. All this, if you please, by the orders of Faustus, who was once so tender-hearted, he would rescue the fly from the spider. What do you think of that?

AZAREL

A truly remarkable exhibition of primal innocence.

MEPHISTOPHELES

Primal innocence? Primitive brutishness. The fellow's grown mischievous as an ape, lecherous as a goat, giddy as a pea-cock, cruel as a cat, and currish as a cross-bred tyke. Since first man fell into sophistication I have found no way to ruin him so effective as his restoration to a state of nature.

AZRAEL

Indeed? Most interesting.

MEPHISTOPHELES

It's the greatest discovery of the age. Though the work it entails is apt to be a little trying.
{*Enter DEVIL, left, with flowering and fruited branch. He hands it to MEPHISTOPHELES, and exit.*}
This kind of nonsense is merely trivial. But when Faustus takes a fancy to do vulgar conjuring tricks——

AZRAEL

Such as?

MEPHISTOPHELES

Such as swallowing a load of hay and a span of horses; or breaking off his own limbs and strewing them about the place like a dissipated daddy-long-legs; or drawing wine from the table-top, to astonish a parcel of drunken louts in a beer-cellar—well! I do feel the whole thing's rather *infra dig.*

AZRAEL (*amused*)

> You are of Lucifer's household. Your professional pride
> must sustain you.
>> {MEPHISTOPHELES *gives a short, vexed laugh. Enter, from Man-
>> sion 2, FAUSTUS, in the body of his transformation, and WAGNER
>> reading a book. WAGNER has aged considerably in the intervening
>> twenty-four years.*}
> Here comes your master, all agog for fresh marvels.

FAUSTUS

> Hey, Mephistopheles! Why are you idling there? How fare
> our troops? Is the siege well begun?

MEPHISTOPHELES

> It is begun.

WAGNER (*sitting apart and reading abstractedly*)

> Fumitory mingled with treacle, and tormentil, to allay the
> fever.

FAUSTUS

> With what success?

MEPHISTOPHELES

> Already the walls of Rome totter at the blast of our cannon.
> By every gunner stands an able fiend to aim the shot and set
> hell-fire to the match. From the bottomless pit, our sappers
> delve their way deep below mine and counter-mine.

FAUSTUS

> Ha!

WAGNER

> Herb of grace is a mithridate to combat the plague.

MEPHISTOPHELES

The Emperor's army go to the assault as though the devil were in them.

FAUSTUS

So they ought, so they ought. What forces have you dispatched?

MEPHISTOPHELES

Halphas, the mighty earl, strides like a stork before his six-and-twenty legions of the damned. And Salmack, lord of corruption, marquess of hell, whose throne is in the sepulchre; where his strokes light, the maggot and the worm make holiday.

WAGNER

Hoarhound, pimpernel and pellitory are good for stinking sores.

MEPHISTOPHELES

Procell, the strong duke, is there, with eight-and-forty legions; Haborin and Labolas and all the captains of destruction.

FAUSTUS

Brave, brave! This news delights me. What joy can equal the swift tumult of war—shock of arms, shouting of men, crash of cannon, the whole world piled together pell-mell in a quick confusion! We must behold it, Mephistopheles. The Emperor is coming. I have promised that thou wilt show him all manner of fine things in a vision.

AZRAEL

So. There will be more work for me and my people.

FAUSTUS

Who is that? Send him away, Mephistopheles. I am afraid
of him. The smell of death is upon his garments.

AZRAEL

I am Azrael, angel of the souls of the dead; and where war
goes, I must follow.

FAUSTUS

Don't talk about death. I don't like it. What are you doing
here?

AZRAEL

I am carrying to Heaven a soul that once was dear to thee.

FAUSTUS

Whose soul?

AZRAEL

Hast thou forgotten Lisa, the little maid that loved thee?

FAUSTUS

Lisa? Is Lisa dead? Wagner, do you hear this?

WAGNER (quietly)

I know it, master. She died in my arms but now.

FAUSTUS

What killed her?

AZRAEL

She went in thy name into all the plague-stricken quarters of
this city, nursing the sick with the skill that Faustus taught
her, when Faustus felt pity for men. The sickness took her
and she died, and her last prayer was for thee.

FAUSTUS

Alas, alas! Poor Lisa. Oh, Wagner, I can never be happy
again. Why am I so vexed and thwarted? I gave all I had for
happiness. I gave—what was it I gave? I have forgotten . . .
I only sought to be happy, and how can I be happy now that
Lisa is gone?

WAGNER

She brought happiness to all who knew her, and that was
her happiness and mine.

MEPHISTOPHELES (to WAGNER)

All the same, you would have done better to take my advice.

WAGNER

Art thou an authority upon happiness, thou shadow of an
immortal grief? Master, I was never wise; but age and time
have instructed me. To aim at happiness is to miss the mark;
for happiness is not an end at all. It is something that comes
of itself, when we are busy about other matters.

FAUSTUS (without heeding him)

Poor, pretty Lisa. She was kind to me. She looked after all
my wants. What will become of me now?

AZRAEL

Thou wilt go to thine own place, Faustus. But her place is with the
angels in Heaven.
{Exit up to Heaven.}

WAGNER (suddenly recalled to himself)

I must work, I must work. So much to do, and so little time,
now that I am all alone to do it. (He wanders away, right,
reading his book.) Yarrow for green wounds; master-wort is
a sovereign remedy for all diseases. . . .
{He sits down and remains, absorbed in his studies.}

FAUSTUS *(inconsolably)*

My heart is broken. Nothing is left in all the world but
sorrow. *(His eye lights on the branch MEPHISTOPHELES is holding,
and his wandering fancy flits off in a new direction.)* That's pretty.
What is it?

MEPHISTOPHELES

Surely you remember. It is the present you wanted to give
to the Empress.

FAUSTUS

Oh, the Empress? She will be here presently. Hark'ee,
Mephistopheles, the Empress is a fair women, a blithe and
buxom lady. She must be mine, d'ye hear me? I must and
will possess her. Thou shalt bring her to me to-morrow.

MEPHISTOPHELES

To-morrow?

FAUSTUS

Yes, to be sure. I say, thou shalt bring her to-morrow.

MEPHISTOPHELES

There will be no to-morrow for you, master.

FAUSTUS

What's that?

MEPHISTOPHELES

Must I remind you of the terms of our bargain? I have
served you diligently these four-and-twenty years. To-night
the compact ends.

FAUSTUS

What then, devil, what then?

MEPHISTOPHELES

Why then you must die, and be forfeit, body and soul, to hell.

FAUSTUS

Death and hell? Death and hell? Don't speak those words. They madden me. I'll not hear them.

MEPHISTOPHELES

Stop your ears and welcome. But die you must and be damned.

FAUSTUS

Never believe it. There's no such thing as death, nor hell neither—save for a few such lubber-fiends as thou, to do the bidding of Faustus. Sin, death, age, sorrow—all that was a foolish dream, and fled like a dream for ever. Death comes with creaking bones and a sick carcase. Look at me, Mephistopheles. Have I aged a hair in four-and-twenty years? Not I. Then what's all this talk of death? It touches me not. I am the everlasting youth of the world. I am John Faustus. (Flourish without.) Here comes the Emperor, with my lady the Empress. Give me that bough. Make haste.
    {Enter the EMPEROR and EMPRESS, attended.}

EMPEROR

Is Dr. Faustus of Wittenberg here in presence?

FAUSTUS

Good morrow and good fortune to your Imperial Majesties. Health, wealth and honour attend your Grace. And on you, most exquisite, beautiful and benign lady, may Venus bestow the plenitude of her favours. Be you ever fair and fruitful as this golden bough, fresh-plucked for your delight from the garden of the Earthly Paradise.

EMPRESS

Thanks, gentle doctor.

EMPEROR

We are much beholden to you. Tell us now. Is this promised spectacle ready, whereof you have reported such marvels?

MEPHISTOPHELES

Whenever you will. Command my master, and he shall command me.

EMPEROR

We know thee, Mephistopheles, as a cunning artificer and a spirit of great ingenuity. What are you able to show us?

FAUSTUS

Whatsoever you please to desire, of things near or far; past, present, or things to come.

EMPEROR

Then let us see and speak with Socrates, the wisest sage of antiquity.

EMPRESS

Oh, no! Socrates was an elderly, ugly monster, with a snub nose and a scolding wife. Show us rather Adonis; or Apollo singing to his lyre, and attended by the nine Muses.

EMPEROR

Nay, madam; I am neither Adonis nor Apollo. Would you make a jealous husband of me?

EMPRESS

Give me leave, I pray you. Indeed, my good lord, I insist.

EMPEROR

Do you so? Then will I demand to look upon fair Helen of Troy, whose beauty set fire to the world. That is a fair revenge, is it not, Dr. Faustus?

FAUSTUS

Your Majesty is more beautiful than ever Helen was.

EMPRESS

Fie, fie, sir. The flattery is too gross.

MEPHISTOPHELES

The truth is, madam, that by a delicate sorcery my master hath had the fair Helen to his paramour. But he grew weary and left her twenty years since, and now has no value for her.

FAUSTUS

Value? What does that mean? Helen was a troublesome baggage.

MEPHISTOPHELES

Man's delight is ever in the unattainable. When he is innocent, he longs for knowledge; when he is grown wise, he hankers after innocence. Between Lilith and Eve, Adam is unfaithful to both, and there is no contenting him.

FAUSTUS (suddenly aggressive)

But, mark you, Helen is mine for all that.

EMPEROR

We would not for the world offend you. Say no more.

MEPHISTOPHELES

Yet your Majesty shall have his will; for every man is fated, once at least in his life, to look on Helen.

WAGNER

Plantain or rosa solis—what herb shall we lay to a corroding ulcer?

EMPEROR

Enough. We will think upon some other device.

EMPRESS

Do you choose, my lord. But I will not hear of Socrates or Diogenes, or any such old, crabbed philosopher.

EMPEROR

Why then, since I am Emperor and hold half the world in fee, let me see Alexander the Great, weeping because he had no more worlds to conquer.

FAUSTUS

Tush, these are trifles. Alexander is dead and his conquests forgotten. I have better than that to show you.
{Enter a SECRETARY OF STATE, with a letter.}

EMPEROR

Anything, so it be diverting. (To the SECRETARY.) How now?

SECRETARY

Here is urgent news, sire, from Rome. Your Imperial armies, leagued with the Constable of Bourbon, have this night attacked the city, with intent to seize the Vatican and overthrow the Pope.
{Sensation.}

EMPEROR

To overthrow the Pope?

EMPRESS

Alas! this is sacrilege!

EMPEROR

How came the news so soon?

FAUSTUS (*eagerly*)

Sire, this is what we would show you. My couriers, sped by a magical device, have brought the message on the wings of the wind. My arms, my arts are at your service. We shall have as merry a battle as ever we had at Pavia.

EMPEROR

This will not do. Who writes the letter?

SECRETARY

The captain of your lanskers.

EMPEROR

Read what he says.

SECRETARY (*reads*)

"The Pope is the Emperor's worst enemy. This war is of his making, and the insult to our master must be avenged. For the honour of God he must be hanged, though I have to do it with my own hand."

EMPRESS

Worse and worse.

EMPEROR (*as though persuading himself*)

True; the old fox has brought it upon himself. He has intrigued against me with France, with Venice and with Milan. He has roused up the Holy League to oppose me— me, that have ever been the champion of the Church. Nevertheless——

FAUSTUS

Why do you hesitate? Sweep him out of the way. You have the power—take all you can and keep it.

EMPEROR

We have never sought for conquest. Yet what is our own by right and inheritance we must and will defend.

MEPHISTOPHELES

Sire, if a poor ignorant devil may venture an opinion, there is but one question here. Who is to be master of Europe? Germany is yours; Spain and the Netherlands are yours. England is rotten with decay; she will truckle to the stronger power. France alone is your foe, and you cannot control France while your hands are tied by Rome. Crush the Pope and make Germany secure against France, and you may be sovereign of the world.

EMPEROR

Security? Yes. Chancellor, what do you say? The Pope is our spiritual sovereign?

CHANCELLOR

Then, sire, let him not meddle with the temporal arm. That belongs to Caesar, and the Emperor is Caesar's heir. The Church that appeals to Caesar's weapons is sold to Caesar already, and must abide the arbitration of Caesar.

MEPHISTOPHELES

Excellent, excellent. "Render unto Caesar——" I couldn't have quoted Scripture better myself.

EMPRESS

Yet how can we prevail, if God be not on our side?

WAGNER

Are we so sure that God takes sides? He sits in the centre like the sun and rules our orbits whether we will or no.

MEPHISTOPHELES

Well spoken, Wagner. God will not care, He makes His
profit either way.

WAGNER

We may dwell on the light side or the dark side. That is all.

FAUSTUS (contemptuously)

Here's a wealth of my astronomy at second-hand.

EMPEROR

Right or wrong; if we attack the Pope the world will con-
demn us. And how then?

MEPHISTOPHELES

Use policy, sir, use policy.

FAUSTUS

I am weary of all this. Let's have the show.

MEPHISTOPHELES (to FAUSTUS)

Master, you are very right. (To the EMPEROR). Say nothing,
know nothing, watch how the battle goes. If your armies are
defeated, hang your generals. If they are victorious, rebuke
them in public and reward them secretly. Deny the deed
and wink at it. Learn to be ignorant, for ignorance is the
master-weapon of policy.

FAUSTUS

You are tedious with your policy.

MEPHISTOPHELES

As to the outcome of the fight, I will answer for it. Dr.
Faustus will assist you by his art. (Aside to the CHANCELLOR.)
And what better ally can you have in war than a profound
scientific knowledge coupled with a total innocence of all
moral responsibility?

CHANCELLOR

You may think such things, but not say them.

EMPEROR

There to the South, under the sun, lies Rome—
Would that the sun's rays, journeying hence, could show us
What his bright eye beholds!

FAUSTUS

Why, so they can
My magical arts to aid.

WAGNER

The camomile
Was consecrate in Egypt to the sun;
It cureth ague and the melancholy.

MEPHISTOPHELES

Turn your back to the light, and look up northward,
Where the pale clouds lie like a silver screen.
See where the shadows waver, cast by the sun,
As spectres move on the Brocken.

EMPEROR

I see! I see!

ATTENDANTS

O wonderful!

EMPEROR

The ramparts of a city—
The tumult of armed men—banners and lances—

FAUSTUS

Now they advance—now they retreat—the gunners
Stand to their cannon—

MEPHISTOPHELES

> They touch the linstock now—

EMPEROR

The brazen mouths belch fire—

EMPRESS

> The smoke rolls over—

FAUSTUS

Up, winds, and send the echo! Let us hear
The terrible voice, the glorious voice of war!
{Confused noise, and chambers shot off within.}

EMPEROR

The wall is breached! Our lanskers storm the gap,
Crying, God save the Emperor!

CHANCELLOR

> Stones and chains
Are hurled upon them!

FAUSTUS

> Haro! still they go forward—

SECRETARY

No, they give ground!

EMPRESS

> Locked to and fro they sway—

EMPEROR

They are repulsed again.

CHANCELLOR

> The town's defenders
Make sortie through the breach.

FAUSTUS

> Now, now our hosts,
The hosts of hell stride out between the armies!

EMPEROR

A smother of smoke hides all.

FAUSTUS

> They march, they march,
The tall, infernal seraphim! O brave!
Raim, that once ruled as a throne in Heaven
Now like a raven spreads his sable pinions
And drives all backward.

MEPHISTOPHELES

> Focalor the duke
On griffin wings hovers before the Romans,
And by his art calls up the inky Styx
Bubbling about their feet; bogs of delusion
Snare them about.

FAUSTUS

> They stumble and go down
Held in the stinking marsh. The water drowns them!

EMPEROR

I see not this—only a mist of blackness
Shot through with flame.

CHANCELLOR

> Ha! the defenders rally!
Rank upon rank they crowd the wall. Our armies
Falter—

EMPEROR

      The day is lost!

MEPHISTOPHELES

                  Strike, Halphas, strike,
Lord of the legions, builder and destroyer
Of towers!
   {*A great explosion.*}

FAUSTUS

      Well done! well done!

EMPEROR

                    A monstrous mine
Bursts in the breach, and blows them all to pieces!
Arms, bodies, stones and fragments, nightmare faces,
And shattered engines tumbled together, falling—

EMPRESS

      O, fearful!

CHANCELLOR

      In! in! in! the town is taken!

EMPEROR

      Our hosts rush on—they carry all before them—

FAUSTUS

      Swords out and forward pikes! The streets run blood,
The horses trample the fallen!

MEPHISTOPHELES

                The Pope is fled
To the castle of Sant' Angelo—

EMPEROR

They surround him—

FAUSTUS

Brands! brands! and fire in the city!

EMPRESS (covering her eyes)

Enough! no more!

MEPHISTOPHELES

Visions away! The Emperor's arms prevail.

CHANCELLOR

Congratulations to your Majesty;
You are master now of Europe.

FAUSTUS

Is the show ended?
I was enjoying myself. Begin again.

MEPHISTOPHELES (briskly)

Nothing more is needed. Your Majesty knows exactly where
you stand. Write quickly now to your general, forbidding
him to attack, and to all your brother sovereigns, explaining
that the thing was done without your knowledge.

EMPEROR (to SECRETARY)

Put the letters in hand immediately.

MEPHISTOPHELES (aside)

Innocence and ignorance, most ravishing and blessed
qualities, what should we do without you? If we have not
set Europe at odds for four hundred years, my name is not
Mephistopheles.

EMPEROR

Will not the Pope take vengeance for this?

MEPHISTOPHELES

Never fear it. He is bound hand and foot. See where he
stalks, a pallid phantom, the sport and puppet of Empire.
{*The Phantom of the* POPE *appears, led in chains by* DEVILS.}

POPE

John Faustus! John Faustus!

FAUSTUS (*shrinking like a whipped cur*)

Touch me not. Spare me. Let me go.

MEPHISTOPHELES

Courage, master. He cannot harm you. . . . There was a
Pope once, scourged Faustus to the heart. He carries the
sting in his memory. . . . Up, I say! What are you grovelling
for?

POPE

Thou fool! This night shall thy soul be required of thee.
{*The* PHANTOMS *pass away.*}

FAUSTUS (*laughing wildly*)

Aha! did you hear that? The old fool dares to threaten me!
Punish him, Mephistopheles! Away, old rogue! I will have
you beaten, tortured, smothered in sulphur! Up, devils, and
after him!

MEPHISTOPHELES

Master, be quiet.

EMPRESS

Pour soul! he is distracted.

MEPHISTOPHELES

Leave him to me. *(He shakes* FAUSTUS *into subjection as one would shake a dog.)* Come now. What will your friends think of you? Never mind the Pope! *(FAUSTUS growls angrily at the name.)* I say, be quiet. Never mind him. *(To the* EMPRESS.*)* Fear nothing, madam. This fit takes him at times, but his bark is worse than his bite. *(To* FAUSTUS.*)* Peace, now. Consider. Is there no other entertainment we can show the Emperor? Some handsome compliment? Some pageant of victory?

FAUSTUS *(all eagerness)*

Yes, yes, I am ready. What would your Majesty like to see?

MEPHISTOPHELES

Master, we will show him the thing he asked for, the longing of his inmost heart. Music, strike up!
  {Music plays.}
The sun if fled, and darkness folds the earth
Like the chill shade that steals before the eclipse.
  *{*WAGNER *springs to his feet, dropping his book with a crash.}*
Rise up, thou star of evening, called by night
Hesperus, but in the morning, Lucifer,
And sometimes Venus, lady of love.

WAGNER

                    O master,
Look to thy soul, the sands are all run out.
  {Enter the vision of HELEN, *veiled and carrying a wreath of laurel.}*

EMPEROR *(rising)*

What wondrous shape is this, that gliding moves
So like a goddess, and in her hand holds forth
The glittering laurel?

MEPHISTOPHELES

                    Learn and mark well her name.
She is all things to all men; and unto thee

The spirit of power, that like the will o' the wisp
Flits on the waters of time, and lures men on
To victory or to death. She is the promise
Of golden phantasy, the worm in the brain,
The song in the soul; she is the world's desire.
Gaze on her face, for men have died for her,
Great cities perished, gallant ships gone down,
Thrones and dynasties crumbled away to dust
For a glance of her eye. She is the unattained,
The unattainable.

HELEN (standing high in the EMPEROR's seat)

    Crowns for the victor, crowns,
Riches and wisdom, honour and glory and blessing.

EMPEROR

O, my heart burns. Unveil, thou wonder of women.

WAGNER

Beware, beware! It is glamour!

MEPHISTOPHELES (throwing back HELEN's veil)

      Have thy will.
Behold the face of Helen.

FAUSTUS (as the EMPEROR springs forward)

     Keep off! She is mine!

EMPEROR

Stand back and let me not!

WAGNER

    Master, forbear!
{FAUSTUS throws WAGNER down. Exit MEPHISTOPHELES,
back.}

EMPEROR

Give place, I say!

EMPRESS

O Heaven!

FAUSTUS (*drawing his sword*)

Look to thyself!

CHANCELLOR

Will you lay hand upon the Emperor?
Treason! treason!
{CROWD *rushes in and surrounds them. In the confusion,* HELEN
is carried up back-stage by the EMPEROR *and the* CHANCELLOR,
*and held in one of the entrances, with her back to the audience. As
she goes, she drops the laurel wreath near* WAGNER. EMPRESS
in the arms of her ladies, left.}

A COURTIER

Vile sorcerer!

SECRETARY

Murderous dog!

CROWD

Down with him! Down!

FAUSTUS

Help, Mephistopheles!
{*His cry momentarily arrests the action.* MEPHISTOPHELES *reappears above Hell-mouth, right, flourishing the bond.*}

MEPHISTOPHELES

Faustus, the four-and-twenty years are past,
My service done. The devil claims his own.

FAUSTUS

Hell and danmation!
{*He is dragged down upon the fore-stage. AZRAEL comes down out of Heaven and enters, left, bearing a black pall.*}
Wagner! Lisa! Christ!
Save me! Have pity!

CROWD

Strike now!

MEPHISTOPHELES

Bondsman of hell,
Die and be damned!

CROWD

Take that!

FAUSTUS

O I am slain!
{*As FAUSTUS falls among the CROWD, there is a loud cry upstage.*}

EMPEROR

She's fled! Helen is vanished! Melted away
Clean from our hands—only her garments left!
O sorcery!
{*He comes down a little, holding HELEN's cloak.*}

AZRAEL (*he is now on the fore-stage, with his back to the audience, and holding the pall spread out*)

Princes and earthly powers
Pass like a pageant, and make room for death.
Cover the face of Faustus.
{*AZRAEL and WAGNER cover FAUSTUS with the pall, and AZRAEL kneels beside the body, still with his back to the audience.*}

WAGNER (rising)

> O dear master,
> Now art thou gone to find reality.
> May God remember all thy willing manhood,
> Not thy refusal. This thy golden dream
> Shall dwell with me; and I will be thine heir,
> Hoping that hope may yet outdo despair.
> > {Exit WAGNER carrying the laurel wreath. The stage empties of
> > all except AZRAEL and MEPHISTOPHELES, who now comes
> > down.}

MEPHISTOPHELES

Thank you, Azrael. I will trouble you for that soul. You
needn't think you can sneak off with it. I saw you. It's
bought and paid for. Here is the bond. Be good enough to
hand it over.

AZRAEL (who has the soul of FAUSTUS in his arms,
concealed in a bag)

Just a moment. Things must be done in an orderly way. The
man is dead, and I have taken his soul in charge. That is my
office. If you think you have any claim on the property,
produce your evidence.

MEPHISTOPHELES (producing the bond)

There you are. Laugh that off.

AZRAEL

It appears to be properly executed. Always supposing your
client's soul was his to sell.

MEPHISTOPHELES

And whose else should it be?

AZRAEL

God's, Who redeemed it.

MEPHISTOPHELES

Nonsense. You can't get away with a legal quibble like that.
The deed's watertight, and you know it.

AZRAEL

Well, you can take the soul on the security of the bond. But
I shall enter a caveat, and appeal to the High Court.
{He hands the bag over.}

MEPHISTOPHELES

You can enter anything you like. Come now, my little
master, my high-and-mighty magician, let's have a look at
you. You've given me trouble enough. Let's see how you like
it when *I'm* the master! Believe me, my friend, I'll make it
hot for you. (He opens the bag and pulls out a BLACK DOG.)
Here! What's this? What's happened to it? You rascally,
cogging angel! You cozening celestial sharp and shyster!
This isn't the right soul!

AZRAEL

It's all the soul he's got.

MEPHISTOPHELES

It's a fraud! I've been tricked! That damned charlatan
Faustus has cheated me. What's the use of a thing like this?

AZRAEL

That's your affair. *Caveat emptor.*

MEPHISTOPHELES

It was a perfectly good soul when I bought it. And now,
look at it!

AZRAEL

It does seem to be rather out of repair. What have you been
doing to it?

MEPHISTOPHELES

    Great Lucifer! I like that. *I* been doing to it?

AZRAEL

    You've had it these twenty-four years. If that's the way you treat the King's property——

MEPHISTOPHELES

    I'll not stand it. God never plays fair. But I've got a clear case. I'll have the law of you——

AZRAEL

    I'll sue you for damages——

MEPHISTOPHELES

    I'll have my rights, I tell you. I will have justice!
    {*Without pause or shift of furniture, the action passes to the next Scene.*}

SCENE IV

The Court of Heaven

{Heaven opens, and the JUDGE appears above.}

JUDGE

Who calls on justice?

MEPHISTOPHELES

                    I, Mephistopheles.
I am defrauded of my rightful due,
Payment for four-and-twenty years of hard
Devoted, scrupulous, vigorous, swift, exacting,
Skilled and assiduous labour, by John Faustus
The conjurer of Wittenberg, and this
Smug-faced angel of yours.

AZRAEL

                       Sir, I protest!
The fraud is all the other way. This fellow
Contracted with John Faustus for his soul,
Payable in exchange for value received,
The bond, post-dated, falling due to-day;
Which soul, I took in charge at Faustus' death
In execution of my official duty,
Lock, stock, and barrel as it stood. He claimed
The same upon his bond, which seemed in order
So far as such things go. I handed over
The goods to him, entering a caveat
In the King's name, as to the ownership,
Since it might well appear the vendor had
No title to give, barter, sell, exchange,
Mortgage or pawn or otherwise dispose of

Crown property. Well and good. But in the interim
(To wit, the four-and-twenty years expired)
This Mephistopheles, by his own act——

MEPHISTOPHELES

That I deny. It was the act of Faustus
Or Azrael, or God, or all of them——

AZRAEL

Had so deformed the soul that it is useless
To God or him, Faustus or any one.
Therefore he claims: and first, against myself
That I did not deliver the true soul
But something substituted; or if I did,
Then against Faustus, for a wilful damage
Executed upon the soul, whereby
He should escape the explicit provision
Made by the bond; lastly, against the Crown,
That if it prove that Faustus or myself
Were acting in this matter as the King's agent,
The Crown may quit the claim. To all of which
I answer by a counter-claim for damage
Done to the goods by Mephistopheles—
A wrong to Faustus, and a clear offence
Against God's peace, His crown and dignity.

JUDGE

Set up my chair of justice in the court
Below there; I will give the cause prompt hearing.
    {The JUDGE comes down.}

MEPHISTOPHELES

Olimoth! Belimoth! (To AZRAEL.) Don't you trouble, sir,
I'll see to this. Lymeck! Bealphares!
    {Enter DEVILS both sides.}
A seat for Justice!
    {Exeunt DEVILS and re-enter with a chair, etc.}
(To AZRAEL.)   This is nothing at all
To all the fetching and carrying, running about,

Materialising and dematerialising
This and that and the other, I've had to do
For Faustus—and of all the troublesome clients
Commend me to him.
    {*The* JUDGE *enters.*}
                        Pray, sir, take your seat.
There is the body of the said John Faustus,
This is the bond, and this the soul in question.
    {*When the* JUDGE *has inspected the* SOUL, *the* DEVILS *take it
    into the wings.*}

JUDGE

Show me the paper.

MEPHISTOPHELES

                        Here. *(Fussily.)* You see it says
"I give my soul"—and "soul" in that connection
Must mean a human soul. I have been in business
Upon this planet several million years,
And it is always so interpreted.
But this alleged——

JUDGE

                        Stop talking, Mephistopheles.
Give me a moment to peruse the terms.
Why! What is this? "Agree to take away
The knowledge of good and evil"? Come now, my poor
Deluded and benighted imp of darkness,
What did you think would happen to the soul
When you did that to it?

MEPHISTOPHELES

                        I did not know;
How should I? Never before, in all my long,
Industrious, strictly dishonourable career,
Have I been put to such a task as that.
It was hard work, but still, I did it.

JUDGE

                              Yes;
Your zeal is your undoing. If I say
"Here is a sword of steel; I give it you
On one condition—that you treat it first
With the most powerful corrosive known
To alchemy"— what will the sword be like
By the time you claim it?

MEPHISTOPHELES

                    Well, but if in good faith
I take and treat the sword as you require,
Not knowing how corrosive acts on steel,
Which yet you knew before you gave the order,
Is that an honest bargain?

AZRAEL

                    And suppose
The sword was borrowed, and belongs in fact
To the armoury of God, what will God say?

JUDGE

You have been swindled, Mephistopheles,
By accident, or by design, your own
Contributory negligence assisting.
Where were your wits? 'Tis true, the foes of God
Are not at any time remarkable
For logic or for common-sense. However,
There must be justice; and the point you urge,
Azrael, is well taken, since all souls
Are God's indeed. Therefore these charges come
To rest on Faustus, who to you, and you,
And to God chiefly, is responsible.
We'll hear the prisoner in his own defence.

MEPHISTOPHELES

Faustus hath made himself into a beast
And has no wit to answer more than a beast.

JUDGE

> Truly; but since, in this high court of Heaven
> Where time is not, the present, past and future
> Are all as one, and answerable together
> Eternally to Him that is eternal,
> I call the prisoner. Wake, thou that sleepest!
> Not as thou art, but as thou wast, John Faustus,
> Rise up and answer at the bar of judgment.
> {*They take away the pall.* FAUSTUS *wakes in his own body.*}

FAUSTUS (*as one dreaming*)

> Whither away, love? O return, return!

MEPHISTOPHELES

> What? Dreaming still on Helen?

FAUSTUS

>   Christ! Christ! Christ!
> They have taken away my Lord these many years,
> And I know not where they have laid Him. Sir, if you know,
> Tell me, for I denied Him, and just now
> I heard the crowing of the cock. How long
> The night has been! And now the dawn is red
> And a great storm coming . . . Hush! for I remember.
> I bartered away my soul for ignorance,
> In ignorance, not knowing what I did.
> There has been cheating somewhere. I was not happy
> Those four-and-twenty years. Something was lost
> That makes for happiness. Yet I seemed to know
> Pleasure of a sort, and pain too—but they slipped
> Like water through my fingers, neither perceived
> Fully, nor remembered fully, nor assessed
> At any quotable value.

JUDGE

>   Value exists
> Not in the object, but the valuing mind;
> The soul's choice makes the value. Therefore ask

This poor brute soul thou madest for thyself
How it doth reckon value.

    {*Here a* DEVIL *shall show* FAUSTUS *the* SOUL *and
retire again.*}

FAUSTUS

                    I was cheated;
I did not bargain for a soul like this,
But for the primal innocence that was Adam's
Before he fell to knowledge. Is it sin
To cancel out a sin? Does God love sin
To set such value on it? Or is He helpless
To undo the past; and did the devil speak truth?

JUDGE

All things God can do, but this thing He will not:
Unbind the chain of cause and consequence,
Or speed time's arrow backward. When man chose
To know like God, he also chose to be
Judged by God's values. Adam sinned, indeed,
And with him all mankind; and from that sin
God wrought a nobler virtue out for Adam,
And with him, all mankind. No soul can 'scape
That universal kinship and remain
Human—no man; not even God made man.
He, when He hung upon the fatal tree,
Felt all the passion of the world pierce through Him,
Nor shirked one moment of the ineluctable
Load of the years; but from the griefs of time
Wrought out the splendour of His eternity.
There is no waste with God; He cancels nothing
But redeems all.

FAUSTUS (*to* MEPHISTOPHELES)

                Serpent, thou didst deceive me!

MEPHISTOPHELES

So Adam said, and Eve; but I spoke truth
To them and thee. I warned thee that the truth

Would but beguile thee, as it beguiles all fools.
Thou askedst, What was I? and I spoke truth;
And who made evil? and I spoke the truth;
And what God was? and there I turned the question
Back upon thee, and thou didst answer it
According to thine own folly; but I spoke truth.

JUDGE

The truth, but not the whole truth, Mephistopheles.
The whole truth is the perfect sphere of Heaven;
The hollow half-truth is the empty dome
That roofs the hall of hell, mocking with echoing
Shards of distorted speech and the fiends' laughter.

MEPHISTOPHELES

Laughter! I tell you I have split my sides!
These wiseacres, that are too clever to see
A plain fact in broad daylight. Up they come,
Sidling and bridling like a fretful horse,
Showing the white of the eye. "What, that a fact,
That tall, black, ugly fence? It can't be true,
There must be some way round—the gate, if you please."
And I am there—Oh, I am always there
To bow, and touch my hat, and take my fee
And open the gate that leads them into the circle,
The ring with the barriers, the closed ring, the place
From which there is no way, no way, no way out.

FAUSTUS

Love would have found the way, if way there were:
"Father, if it be possible, let this cup
Pass from Me." But it was not possible, never
Has been nor will be possible. Over the fence
Is the only road. For all the by-ways run
Down to the circle, the closed circle of self
From which there is no way out.

JUDGE

There is no way out.

110

MEPHISTOPHELES (sings)

> Jump little man,
> As high as you can;
> The way across
> Is by thorn and cross;
> But the only way round
> Leads into the pound,
> So hey, so ho,
> And over you go.

AZRAEL

You are too noisy. Silence in the court
The prisoner waits for judgment.

MEPHISTOPHELES

> Yes, and I
Wait for my fee, which has been tampered with.
Here is the bond: "I, Faustus, give my soul
For such and such considerations"—all
Duly fulfilled by me; but where's the soul?
That thing there, which you flatter by the name,
I have no use for; it is not as specified.
If there is justice in this court at all
The devil must have his due.

JUDGE (to FAUSTUS)

> You hear the charge
Preferred against you, on two counts. Imprimis:
That you did sell a soul for which Christ died;
A crime against God's crown. Next, that the price,
Promised in God's true gold, was paid in fact
With coin debased and worthless; a civil trespass
Against this gentlemen. What have you to say?

FAUSTUS

I must admit the trespass, and the crime
That caused the trespass. I have no defence
Save ignorance; yet ignorance was itself

111

The very prize for which the crime was done;
Nor yet is ignorance a defence in law.
Speak thou, O righteous judge, for I am silent.

JUDGE

Poor, empty vessel whence the wine was spilt,
What shall we do with thee? Listen to judgment.
For this last time, God gives thee back again
The power to choose, weighing the good and evil—
A fearful option; yet no other course
Can justice take, since here thou standest bound
In thine own blood, and no remorse of thine
Can raze one jot or tittle from the law.
Hear, then, the dread alternative of choice;
And first, wilt thou, with that dumb changeling soul,
Incapable alike of hell or heaven,
Wander for evermore between the worlds
Unblest, undamned, unknowing?

FAUSTUS

                              Nor blest nor damned?
Merciful God, what kind of doom is this?

JUDGE

A gentle doom; sorrow shall never touch thee,
Nor pain, nor any question vex thee more;
Yea, though thy loss be wider than the world,
Or than a thousand thousand worlds at once,
Thou shalt not feel nor know it.

FAUSTUS

O, what loss?

JUDGE

                A loss beyond all loss: to live content
Eternally, and never look on God;
Never behold the wonder of His face
Fiery with victory, bright above the burning

112

Wings of the cherubim; never to hear the loud
Exultation of trumpets shatter the sky
For the Lamb's marriage-feast; nor drink the wine
Of God; nor feel the glad earth thrill to the tread
Of the tall, strong, unresting angels' feet;
Nor know the dream of desire, that is beyond
All happiness; nor ever more to find
Beauty in sunlight, or the flowery fields,
Or in man's heart; nor ever laugh again.

FAUSTUS

No, no, no, no!

JUDGE

     Does ignorance not suffice thee?
Wilt thou have knowledge after all, John Faustus?
Take back thy soul, then, and fulfil the bond;
Go down with Mephistopheles to hell,
And through the bars of those relentless gates
Gaze on the glory of the Lord far off
And know that He is terrible and just.

FAUSTUS

No choice but this?

JUDGE

      No other choice at all.

FAUSTUS

Either to lose God and not know the loss,
Nor even to remember God exists;
Or see the glories that I may not share,
And in the sharp hell of a lost desire
Burn on unquenchably.

JUDGE

     So stands the choice.

FAUSTUS

O lost, lost, either way!

MEPHISTOPHELES

Excuse my laughter;
Justice hath pinned thee now in a cleft stick.
Writhe, my good friend, my toad beneath the harrow;
'Twill serve thee little, but no matter—squirm
For my amusement. How do you like this game?
You're playing with cogged dice, cully—all sides alike.
Lend me an angel, we'll toss for it; heads I win
And tails you lose. If you call "God!" and win,
Then I win you; and if you lose the throw,
Then you lose God; why then, call "tails," and get
The tail of the dog there. Maybe this will teach you
To play chuck-farthing with your soul!

FAUSTUS

I stand
Between the devil and the deep seas of God
On a road that leads nowhither. This is strange—
The love of God urges my feet towards hell,
The devil that seeks to have me flings me back
Into God's arms. Are you two allies, then,
Playing into each other's hands, and grinning
Friendship across my frontiers? I will have
The truth of this, although the stink reek up
And blast the airs of Heaven! Thou, Mephistopheles,
Answer again, and this time all the truth,
Art thou God's henchman or His master? Speak!
Who made thee?

MEPHISTOPHELES

God, as the light makes the shadow.

FAUSTUS

Is God, then evil?

MEPHISTOPHELES

　　　　　　God is only light,
And in the heart of the light, no shadow standeth,
Nor can I dwell within the light of Heaven
Where God is all.

FAUSTUS

　　　　　What art thou, Mephistopheles?

MEPHISTOPHELES

　　I am the price that all things pay for being,
The shadow on the world, thrown by the world
Standing in its own light, which light God is.
So first, when matter was, I was called Change,
And next, when life began, I was called Pain,
And last, when knowledge was, I was called Evil;
Nothing myself, except to give a name
To these three values, Permanence, Pleasure, Good,
The Godward side of matter, life and knowledge.

FAUSTUS

　　Thus far, then, have I come to learn the truth
I taught my servant, many years ago:
"The sun can cast no shade; only the dark
Dead body of earth or moon can make eclipse
Of his perpetual radiance." Thus I told him,
Being blind to my own parable; but he,
Knowing no syllable of sun or moon,
Walked in the light of the true innocence
To the end I sought for. Pity my blindness, sir,
For His dear sake that healed the blind and cast
The devils out——

MEPHISTOPHELES

　　　　　Hast thou learned nothing yet?
He'll not reverse the past. The past is here
And thou must answer it.

FAUSTUS

> O, by the Name
> And power of Him that harrowed hell——

MEPHISTOPHELES

> Thou fool!
> Thou juggling sorcerer! Thinkest thou with those
> Same words wherewith thou once did'st conjure me
> To conjure justice?

FAUSTUS

> Devil, thou didst speak truth,
> And with thine own truth will I choke thee now
> To the deep of thy false throat. Not in the words
> Is power, but in the faith of him that speaks,
> And in the person of the very Christ
> In Whom stands all the meaning of creation.
> Words? They are rags, tags, fluttering remnants blown
> Along the winds of fancy; only in Him
> Is neither variableness nor shadow of turning.
> Sir, I beseech thee, as thou are all truth,
> Answer me truly; in this desperate choice
> What would God have me do?

JUDGE

> I may not tell thee.
> Only the knowledge of the good and evil
> Gained once by sin, by double sin rejected,
> Restored again by grace, is granted thee
> For guidance. Thou must choose and choose alone.

MEPHISTOPHELES

> Why, this is better than a circus! Round
> And round again till you're giddy, faster and faster
> Round the closed circle. I met you first in a circle——
> You should know something of circles. You're well inside,
> Dodging the ring-master there, with the hoop in his hand
> And the lash at your heels. Faster and faster, Faustus,

Round and round, and then—the crack of the whip
And through the hoop you go. So, Faustus, choose
In the devil's name.

AZRAEL

                    In the name of the most high God
Choose, Faustus, and for ever.

FAUSTUS

                         I have chosen.
I will go down with Mephistopheles
To the nethermost pit of fire unquenchable
Where no hope is, and over the pathless gulf
Look up to God. Beyond that gulf I may
Never pass over, nor any saint nor angel
Descend to me. Nevertheless, I know
Whose feet can tread the fire as once the water,
And I will call upon Him out of the deep,
Out of the deep, O Lord.

JUDGE

                         Art now so bold
To call down God, thou that aforetime didst
With cowardly conjurations call up devils?
Then tell me: art thou able to be baptised
With Christ's most bitter baptism, or to drink
The cup that all His shuddering mortal flesh
Shrank from, yet drank, down to the dark dregs, driven
By the strong spirit?

FAUSTUS

                    I dare not say I am able.
Yet I say this: that nothing thou canst do
Shall threat me from the quest of Christ eternal.
Yea, though thou stand with thy keen sword made bare
To keep me from Him, and have at thy command
In ninefold rank the terrible hosts of Heaven,
Yet will I seek Him. If I go down to hell
He is there also; or if He stand without,

My hands shall batter against hell's brazen gates
Till the strong bars burst asunder and let Him in.
Then will I seize Him, then fall down before Him,
Cling to His garments, hold Him fast by the feet,
Cry in His ear, "I will not let Thee go
Except Thou bless me. Even the unjust judge
Heard the poor widow, and Thou shalt hear me!
Spare not Thy rod, for Thou hast borne the rod,
Quench not Thy fire, for Thou didst pass through fire,
Only be with me!"

MEPHISTOPHELES

     This is brave indeed!

FAUSTUS

Mock me not, nothingness; I have found courage
In Him that never feared to look on sorrow,
And though He slay me, I will trust in Him.

MEPHISTOPHELES

Then, Faustus, thou art mine!

FAUSTUS

        Thine here and now,
But wheresoever and whensoever, God's.
Sir, I am ready.

MEPHISTOPHELES

    Come on, my violent friend.

JUDGE

The kingdom of Heaven suffereth violence,
And violent men may take it by assault
In the last breach of despair. Thus all things come
To their own place at last, the tares to the burning
And the good grain to God.
  (To MEPHISTOPHELES.) Thou hast claimed thine own,
It is thine. Burn it. Touch not my good grain,

118

I shall require it at thy hand some day;
And for thou knowest that thy time is short,
Be diligent.

MEPHISTOPHELES

     I'll warrant thee for that.
Open the gates there!
  {Hell-mouth opens.}

JUDGE

      Faustus, look on me;
Through the harsh mask of judgment read my soul,
And when I meet thee at the gates of hell,
Know me again.

FAUSTUS

    Slay me, but leave me not.

JUDGE

Lo! I will never leave thee, nor forsake thee
Even to the world's end. Take him, Mephistopheles,
And purge him throughly, till he find himself,
As I have found him mine. God is not robbed;
And I will bring mine own as I did sometime
From the deep of the sea again.

FAUSTUS

      From the deep of the sea.
 {FAUSTUS is led away by MEPHISTOPHELES to Hell, AZRAEL
 and the DOG accompanying him. The JUDGE goes up into Heaven.}

DEVILS (below)

Deep calleth unto deep with the noise of the cataracts.

AZRAEL

Out of the deep have I called unto Thee, O Lord; Lord,
hear my voice.

DEVILS (below)

Sheol is naked before Him, and Abaddon hath no covering.

AZRAEL

O let Thine ears consider well the voice of my complaint.

DEVILS (below)

They lie in the hell like sheep, death gnaweth upon them;
their beauty shall consume in the sepulchre.

AZAREL

But God hath delivered my soul from the place of hell, for
He shall receive me.
{The JUDGE being now come up into Heaven, the gates are opened
with a great light. FAUSTUS at Hell's mouth sees the glory of
Heaven.}

ANGELS (above)

Return, return, O Shulamite; return, return, that we may
look upon thee.

AZRAEL

If any man's work shall be burned, he shall suffer loss.

DEVILS (below)

Where their worm dieth not, and their fire is not quenched.

ANGELS (above)

But he himself shall be saved, yet so as by fire.
{FAUSTUS follows MEPHISTOPHELES into Hell,
and the DOG with him. Hell-mouth is shut upon them.}

CHORUS (while AZRAEL returns into Heaven)

Multitudes, multitudes in the valley of decision; for the day
of the Lord is near in the valley of decision.

That which the palmer-worm hath left hath the locust
    eaten; and that which the locust hath left hath the
    canker-worm eaten.
A fire devoureth before them, and behind them a flame
    burneth.
Multitudes, multitudes, in the valley of decision.

Rend your heart and not your garments, and turn unto the
    Lord your God;
And I will restore unto you the years which the locust hath
    eaten.
Multitudes, multitudes—I beheld, and lo! a great multitidue,
Ten thousand times ten thousand, and thousands of
    thousands.

Worthy is the Lamb that was slain to receive power, and
    riches, and wisdon, and strength, and honour, and
    glory, and blessing;
Blessing and honour, and glory, and power, be unto Him
    that sitteth upon the throne, and unto the Lamb, for
    ever and ever. Alleluia. Amen.

FINIS

HE THAT
SHOULD COME

A NATIVITY PLAY IN ONE ACT

NOTE TO PRODUCERS

HE THAT SHOULD COME was originally written for broadcasting, and its adaptation for the stage has presented certain difficulties, owing to the difference between the two media. The main dialogue seemed to require little alteration; the trouble begins with the background and subsidiary characters.

The intention of the play is to show the birth of Christ against its crowded social and historical background, and for that purpose it was necessary to make real to the audience the bustling and variegated life of an autonomous province in the great, sprawling, heterogeneous Roman Empire of the first century. The inn was to be shown crowded with as many and various types as possible—the orthodox Pharisee, with his rigidly national religious views; the Hellenised Jew, with his liberal outlook influenced by contact with Rome; the Greek, with his intellectual pliability and sceptical detachment; the trader, treading warily on thorny political ground and anxious to give offence to nobody; the peasant, earning a precarious livelihood amid the hurly-burly of conflicting forces perpetually threatening his small security; behind them all, the ruthless tyranny of a self-made Oriental despot, ruling a strange mixed province of strict Jews in the south and fierce heathen tribes in the north; and behind him again, the iron strength of Rome, legal, military, and imperial, caring nothing for internal politics or religious disputes so long as her tributaries kept the peace and paid the taxes.

To obtain this effect, the scene was laid, not with particular reference to the traditional cave at Bethlehem, but in an Oriental inn of the usual kind, consisting of a two-storied rectangular building surrounding an open courtyard, somewhat after the style of a college quandrangle. In the centre of the courtyard was a raised platform, on which the travellers sat or lay, surrounded by their luggage. The ground floor of the building consisted of a series of vaulted stables carrying the chambers on the first floor, over which was a flat roof. The inn had a gate, which was barred at night against marauders. The inn is supposed to be situated on the road going up from Bethlehem to Jerusalem.

It thus became possible to introduce all the necessary characters quite plausibly into this common courtyard. For the purpose of a broadcast, the crowded condition of the inn was sufficiently indicated by introducing a few allusions to the throng of travellers and by fading in a babble of voices at appropriate points in the dialogue. Attention was easily focused on one point or another of the scene by conveying the suggestion of the character picking his way among the assembled travellers, and by inserting a line to announce his arrival at the gate, the stable, the Centurion's post, and so forth.

This scene, so excellently suitable for a broadcast, at once offers difficulties in the theatre, where the crowd of travellers has not merely to be indicated, but to be seen in action and kept continually on the stage. Having once introduced the characters, you cannot move them off and leave the stage clear, because it is the whole point of the story that the inn was crowded to suffocation and that there *was* no clear space. In consequence, the stage being thus crowded and obliged to remain crowded, it becomes very difficult to move the actors naturally from one point to another, or to give the "background characters" anything sensible to do without distracting attention from the speakers. A subsidiary difficulty was to being the various groups, as they became important to the action, into a sufficiently commanding position and not leave them isolated up-stage or blocked in inconvenient doorways to right and left.

I have coped with these difficulties as well as I could, bearing in mind that the play may be acted by repertory or amateur companies having at their disposal stages of widely varying dimensions and lighting equipment. The play as here arranged allows for the largest stage and the largest company that are likely to be available. There are fifteen characters necessary for the performance of the dialogue; to these I have added nine subsidiary characters to bring the cast up to twenty-four. These, with a proper allowance of baggage and other properties, should be enough to produce a quite convincing crowd on a stage of reasonable dimensions. The actual "crowding-space" of the stage will be governed by the size of the central rostrum, where this is available, and the scenery or curtains can be brought in accordingly.

Where the stage is insufficiently large to accommodate the full cast, the minor characters can be cut down at will, and the "background" dialogue altered to fit the situation. The guiding principle to be taken is to ask: How many people will give an effect of real crowding on this particular stage? and to work from that figure. Where the smallness of the stage or of the available company requires the cast to be limited to the fifteen principal characters, the Landlady's call for a midwife can be answered from off-stage, as though from the upper storey of the inn.

In the absence of built scenery, the play can very suitably be performed in curtains; an inner set of these can be bunched so as to suggest the archways alluded to in the text. The stage directions allow for either one or two archways on either side, according to the depth of the stage. Where there are two, the directions "right" and "left" should be taken to refer to the lower entrances and the directions in brackets (R.U.) and (L.U.) to the upper entrances.

If the play is performed in a church without scenery or curtains, it is suggested that the entrance to the choir should be screened off and opened to display the tableau of the Holy Family. The exits right and left can then be suitably made into the aisle or transept as the case may be, whose arches will supply the appropriate suggestion.

What is done with the Kings during the main action of the play depends upon the means at the producer's disposal. I have made one or two suggestions, according as the building is furnished with one or more sets of front curtains and with more or less elaborate front-of-house lighting. If the play is given in a church without curtain, the Kings might very suitably enter from the west door, through the darkened nave, and be lit by a single spot or a strong electric torch till the time comes to light the whole scene. It would then be symbolically appropriate that they should make their exit eastward, if possible, up either side of the choir towards the Sanctuary, with the light of a torch going before them to represent the Star.

The action of the play should take about an hour. If it is found too long, the Greek Gentleman's Song and the second verse of the Soldiers' Marching Song may be cut. In the original broadcast the long speeches of the Kings were also omitted; but this cut is not recommended. As accompaniment to the songs, a harp, lute, guitar (if that is the best available), or other plucked string instrument will give the right effect; orchestral or organ accompaniments are quite unsuitable. A piano would do at a pinch; a harpsichord still better.

The whole effect and character of the play depend on its being played in an absolutely natural and realistic style. Any touch of the ecclesiastical intonation or of "religious unction" will destroy its intention. The whole idea in writing it was to show the miracle that was to change the whole course of human life enacted in a world casual, inattentive, contemptuous, absorbed in its own affairs and completely unaware of what was happening: to illustrate, in fact, the tremendous irony of history. It may be found advisable to make this point clear to the actors before they start, lest some preconceptions as to what is or is not "reverent" in a Nativity Play should hamper the freedom of their performance. I feel sure that it is in the interests of a true reverence towards the Incarnate Godhead to show that His Manhood was a real manhood, subject to the common realities of daily life; that the men and women surrounding Him were living human beings, not just characters in a story; that, in short, He was born, not into "the Bible," but into the world. That an audience will take the play in this spirit is proved to me by the various letters I received after the first broadcast. As one man in a country village put it, "It's nice to think that people in the Bible were folks like us." And another correspondent: "None of us realised before how much we had just accepted the story without properly visualising it. It . . . brought home to us as never before the real humanity of Jesus." There will always be a few voices raised to protest against the introduction of "reality" into religion; but I feet that the great obstacle in the path of Christianity to-day is that to so many it has become unreal, shadowy, "a tale that it told," so that it is of the utmost importance to remind people by every means in our power that the thing actually happened— that it is, and was from the beginning, closely in contact with real life.

I found that the broadcasting company really enjoyed playing in this little piece of "real-life" drama, and hope that it will prove itself "good theatre" in a different medium. Since I have had no chance to try out the adaptation with actors upon a stage, I shall be very glad if producers will let me or my agents know how it works out in practice, and what devices their ingenuity has used to get over the obvious "snags" in presentation, so that, if necessary, I may revise the text in the light of their experience.

DOROTHY L. SAYERS.

He That Should Come was first performed in the original broadcast version on the London National Transmission from Broadcasting House on Christmas Day, 1938, with the following cast:

CASPAR	Harcourt Williams
MELCHIOR	William Devlin
BALTHAZAR	Robert Adams
MERCHANT	Henry Longhurst
GREEK GENTLEMAN	Robert Farquharson
PHARISEE	Alan Wheatley
CENTURION	Gordon McLeod
LANDLORD	Philip Wade
LANDLADY	Marjorie Fielding
JOSEPH	Patrick Curwen
MARY	Gwen Catley
JEWISH GENTLEMAN	Raf de la Torre
1ST SHEPHERD	Wallace Evenett
2ND SHEPHERD	Frederick Peisley
3RD SHEPHERD	Pat Laffan

Barry Faber, Angela Kirk and the B.B.C. Singers

The Music composed by ROBERT CHIGNELL

Producer: VAL GIELGUD

The present version has been adapted for Stage Performance by the author.

DRAMATIS PERSONÆ

Persons of the Prologue and Epilogue

CASPAR, King of Chaldea, an aged man.

MELCHIOR, King of Pamphylia, a man in the
   prime of life.

BALTHAZAR, King of Ethiopia, a young Negro.

Persons of the Play

THE JEWISH MERCHANT, a stout man with a
   plummy voice.

THE PHARISEE, a tall, thin and severe man.

THE YOUNG GREEK GENTLEMAN, a suave young
   man, with a foreign accent.

THE JEWISH GENTLEMAN, the "Oxford Graduate"
   of the period.

THE ROMAN CENTURION, the very best type
   of non-commissioned officer.

THE LANDLORD, a square-built, husky-voiced
   person, with a wholesome terror of the law.

THE LANDLADY, a harassed woman with a shrill
   voice.

JOESPH, a mild, courteous man, with the plain dignity
   of the skilled artisan.

MARY, a serene, sweet-voiced woman, with an air of
   great stillness about her.

1ST SHEPHERD, an elderly peasant.

2ND SHEPHERD, a middle-aged peasant.

3RD SHEPHERD, a young peasant.

Minor Personages

Two Roman Soldiers—A Husband and Wife—A Father,
   Mother and Little Boy—A Manservant—A Maidservant.

PROLOGUE

*{The Prologue is played upon the fore-stage. If there is a front
curtain as well as tableaux curtains, it rises to discover* MELCHIOR.
If not, MELCHIOR *should enter in darkness before the curtain, and
a steel spot be gradually turned up to reveal him, sitting left of stage.}*

MELCHIOR *(sings to the tinkling of a lute)*
    High upon the holy tree
      (Whither away, love?)
    Dragon-guarded ceaselessly
      (Whither away?)
    There hangs the splendour sought of old,
    The lamb, the ram, the fleece of gold
      (Colchis, O Colchis,
      Give me my heart again!)
  {Enter CASPAR. *He speaks out of the darkness, right.}*

CASPAR

 What traveller is that,
 Sitting and singing beside the desert fountain,
 Challenging with his frail music
 This blinding silence of silver midnight,
 Brighter than moonlight, whiter than sunlight,
 This unaccustomed miracle of sevenfold starlight?

MELCHIOR *(rising)*

 I am a Greek,
 Born in the West, on the shores of the Mediterranean,
 A European, in fact. I am not afraid of a thing
 Merely because it is unaccustomed. Our instinct
 Is to challenge destiny. That is why I am here.
 There is a muttering among the oracles,
 A song in the poets' mouths. They tell of a child
 That shall shake off the iron yoke of necessity,

Bring back the golden age and the brave Saturnian reign.
He hath set up his sceptre in the sky; very well;
It is my duty to find out the truth about this;
I am a ruler, I owe my people the truth;
And on my people's behalf I have ridden hither,
Melchior, King of Pamphylia, surnamed "the Just,"
Following the Star.

CASPAR *(coming forward into the light)*

I am an astrologer; I have watched from the high towers
Nightly the signs of heaven stride
Through the houses of fate in the turning horoscope.
I have seen this new star turn and burn
Slowly out of the east, leaping from cusp to cusp,
Till now it sits ruling the house of life;
And I have asked myself what god should be born
From this astonishing conjunction. Therefore am I come,
Caspar, King of Chaldea, surnamed "the Wise,"
Following the Star.

MELCHIOR

Listen! the sound of bells—
Another traveller comes, riding upon a camel,
With a train of swift camels. His face is as the night,
His eyeballs glint white in the night of his face. Who's there?
    {Enter BALTHAZAR, right, and speaks out of the darkness.}

BALTHAZAR

Out of the darkness, out of the desert,
Beyond the secret springs of the Nile
I have seen the fire of desire flare in the zenith
Scaring the crocodiles under the shadow of the pyramids.
The dusky gods have trembled, the witch-dancers are
    struck down
In the midst of their dances.
A cry is gone up in the halls of the dead, from the seven
    gates of the dead,
The cry of Isis over Osiris slain,
The birth-cry of Horus.

This is the end or else the beginning of all things,
And sorrow either way, between a cry and a cry;
> {*He comes into the light.*}

Therefore I come, seeking the soul of sorrow,
Balthazar, King of Ethiopia, surnamed "the Servant,"
Following the Star.

MELCHIOR

Yonder it stands, and yonder, by my reckoning,
The City of Jerusalem, a twelve-days' journey hence.

CASPAR

Strangely are we met, Wisdom, Justice, and Service,
Following the Star, seeking we know not what.

BALTHAZAR (*standing between them*)

Magi, my brothers, let us take counsel of the crystal—
I hold it in my dark hand, shining against the darkness of
> my hand;

Let the crystal display to us what shall be the end of the
> journey.
> {*He kneels down.*}

CASPAR

Will he come, will he speak at last, the ultimate wisdom,
The unalterable truth behind and above the appearance?
I have studied all the philosophies, and now I am old;
Every day I care less about life and death, sorrow and
> happiness—

I ask only that what we see shall correspond to something,
Beautiful or terrible, but constant in some way or other.
We build the house of thought, stone upon stone,
And just as we have finished the topmost pinnacle
There comes a grinning doubt and pulls away the founda-
> tion.

One has to assume something before one can think at all,
If it is only the validity of one's own thinking,
Or one's immediate perceptions,
Or the numerical proposition that two and two make four.

Give me a single integer and I will build up the universe,
Star upon flaming star, and the singing orbits of planets,
And the springing sap, and the life in the blood, and
    splendour,
Beauty and love and grief and the promise of immortality—
Only, it is from the universe that I deduce the integer
From which to deduce the universe again;
And thus all knowledge is only a vicious circle
Ceaselessly spinning upon the axis of nothing.
Nor can I even be sure that everything,
Including myself, is nothing,
Since it is in myself that I flnd the all and the nothing;
And it may be that nothingness is in itself an illusion,
The last illusion of all.
    {CASPAR kneels.}

MELCHIOR

I will accept the illusions;
I do not mind whether they are illusions or not,
I am not interested in dogma, I want a religion that works;
What I look for is good government,
A reasonable way of life, within the terms of the illusion.
If there is nothing at the end of it, be it so—there is nothing;
But in the meantime, can we not achieve a little decency,
A little dignity,
A pattern of some kind, such as we make so easily
For a curtain or a cornice, which does not matter at all,
But cannot make for our lives, which matter a great deal,
Or, at any rate, seem to matter? Always we hope for a
    formula,
The master-word, the philosopher's stone, the elixir of life,
The abracadabra that settles everything—
The formula of empire, the formula of liberty,
The formula of isolation, the formula of collective security,
The formula of discipline, the formula of self-expression,
And all the rest of it.
Always we are disappointed, always there are complications,
There does not seem to be any simple rule
To make things go smoothly.
We have wasted too much time in quarrelling and asking
    questions;

Let us put our trust in a personality
Capable of commanding our loyalty—strength
And leadership, and calm hands ordering everything,
And the government shall be upon his shoulder, lord of
   lords, and king of kings.
    {MELCHIOR *kneels*.}

BALTHAZAR

How much you need to content you!
The wisdom that sets the soul beyond the reach of suffering,
The power to abolish suffering. I am more humble;
I do not mind being ignorant and unhappy—
All I ask is the assurance that I am not alone,
Some courage, some comfort against this burden of fear and pain.
I am a servant, born of the seed of Ham,
The oppressed, the accurst;
My skin is black with the punishing fury of the sun.
About my palaces the jungle creeps and whines,
Famine and plague are my fireside companions,
And beyond the circle of the fire, the glare of hungry eyes.
The lion sits by the water-hole, where the women go down
   to wash,
In the branches crouches the leopard.
I look out between the stragling branches of the vine and
   see
Fear in the east, fear in the west; armies
And banners marching and garments rolled in blood.
Yet this is nothing, if only God will not be indifferent,
If He is beside me, bearing the weight of His own creation;
If I may hear His voice among the voices of the vanquished,
If I may feel His hand touch mine in the darkness,
If I may look upon the hidden face of God
And read in the eyes of God
That He is acquainted with grief.

CASPAR

Gather the rays of the Star into the crystal.

MELCHIOR

Look, and see the shape of things afar off.

BALTHAZAR

Listen, and hear the shadows speak in the crystal.
{*A murmur of movements and voices behind the tableaux curtains
or gauzes.*}

CASPAR

See! the light stirs and blurs to a pale cloud in the crystal—

MELCHIOR

Like an opal, with green fire darting and parting at the core!

BALTHAZAR

Look and listen! the life of the world is born in the heart of
the crystal.
{*The spot is gradually dimmed down upon the THREE KINGS,
who may then make their exit in the black-out, or, if preferred, they
may remain upon the stage throughout the action of the play.*

*If gauzes are available, the lights behind them will be brought up
slowly on the dimmers as the spot fades during the KINGS' last
three lines, and the gauzes taken up in succession during the
opening conversation in the inn.*

*Where there are no gauzes, the tableaux curtains will be opened at
cue on the fully-lit scene.*

*SUGGESTED LIGHTING: Steel in the front spots; blue and white
in No. 3 batten; steel arena flood on check centre for star over stable;
amber flood shining down staircase left (L.U.) and steel flood
through doorway to gate, right; red light in braziers, reinforced by
spots if necessary. The impression to be conveyed is of an
unroofed courtyard on a brilliant star-light night.*

*The Stable of the Nativity can be lit by a white batten, or by a
couple of baby spots centred upon the HOLY CHILD.*}

{*The voices of the travellers are heard before the curtains are
opened. The four following pages must be played at top speed.*}

MERCHANT

Landlord! Landlord!

ANOTHER VOICE *(fading off, left)*

Three of us and six servants, and see that the brown mule gets a good rub down.

PHARISEE

Landlord! Landlord!

MANSERVANT

T'ch, t'ck! Git over there!

MERCHANT

Held up twice between here and Jericho. What the Government thinks its doing. . . .

1ST SOLDIER

Best of three!

2ND SOLDIER

My belt against your Persian dagger.

JEWISH GENTLEMAN

Look sharp, my lad, with that jug of wine.

MANSERVANT

Yes, sir! Yes, sir! Coming in a minute.

WIFE

Really, Ezra, am I to stand here all night?
   {*The curtains open. The centre of the stage is occupied
   by a rectangular platform, its down-stage edge lying just
   behind the curtain line. A passage runs round the back
   and both sides at stage level. At the back are three archways,
   leading to the stables; their entrances (R.B., C.B. and L.B.) are
   concealed by rough hangings of sacking. Similar archways, at
   the sides of the stage, lead, on the right to the gateway of the
   inn, on the left to a staircase going up to the roof. (NOTE.—If
   the depth of the stage permits, there may be two of these*

*entrances either side, in which case the lower right entrance will
lead to the gate, and the upper left to the stairs.) Behind the
centre archway at the back is the Stable of the Nativity, the floor of
which is raised somewhat above the level of the platform. Both platform and passage-way are obstructed by baggage of every description
—mattresses, saddle-bags, saddles, cooking utensils, and so forth.
On the right, the GREEK GENTLEMAN has just entered, and is
working his way centre. Near right entrance sprawl a couple of
ROMAN SOLDIERS, entertaining themselves with a dice-box and a
large pot of beer. Well down, and a little right of centre, the
PHARISEE is sitting, with the LANDLORD in attendance. Just
above centre, a PEASANT FATHER and MOTHER have established
themselves with their LITTLE BOY; a MAIDSERVANT is filling
their pitcher with water and giggling at FATHER. Right of centre
the respectable HUSBAND and WIFE are standing surrounded by
luggage, and looking rather helpless. Above and left of them stands
the MERCHANT, and a little above between them and the family
party stands the ROMAN CENTURION, checking over the papers of
the JEWISH GENTLEMAN. Right back a MANSERVANT is carrying
a bundle of fodder into the stable. All through the opening dialogue
the PHARISEE sits severely silent, reading a scroll.}*

HUSBAND

Of course not, my dear. *(He beckons to the MAIDSERVANT.)*
Here, girl, here! *(The GIRL is being chucked under the chin by the
FATHER, and pays no attention.)*

MAIDSERVANT

Give over, now, do!

LANDLADY *(entering left (L.U.), shrilly)*

Now then, you lazy baggage! Water and towels for the
party upstairs.

MAIDSERVANT

Yes, madam. *(She hurries off, left (L.U.).)*

HUSBAND *(trying in vain to detain her)*

The service in these inns is disgraceful!

WIFE

Is there nobody here to attend to a lady?

LANDLORD *(coming up-stage)*

Wife, here's a lady wants you.

LANDLADY

Gentleman upstairs wants these cleaned. *(She dumps a cloak and a pair of boots into his arms. He takes them off, right (R.U.).)* Yes, madam? *(She attends to WIFE.)*

MANSERVANT *(coming down to JEWISH GENTLEMAN with wine)*

Sorry to keep you waiting, sir. We're run off our feet with the rush.

BOY

Mother! Mother! I want a piece of cake.
　　{CENTURION *goes centre and speaks to* GREEK GENTLEMAN.}

MOTHER

Cake, indeed! You'll wait till supper's ready.

GREEK GENTLEMAN

Native of Bethlehem? Heaven forbid! We're going on to Jerusalem. *(He comes down to MERCHANT.)*

FATHER *(catching MANSERVANT as he returns centre)*

Give us a hand with the pack-saddle, can't you? *(They go up towards stable, back (L.B.). The CENTURION has meanwhile crossed right, and is watching the SOLDIERS at their game.)*

1ST SOLDIER

The gods to aid *(Throws dice.)* Venus, by Bacchus!

2ND SOLDIER

Curse it! You've cleaned me out. *(Drinks.)*

1ST SOLDIER

That's no reason to swill all the beer. *(Snatches pot from him. Scuffle.)*

WIFE

Find us a nice quiet spot, away from those drunken soldiers. {*Her HUSBAND leads her across left, above MERCHANT and his baggage.*}

MANSERVANT *(off, back)*

Steady, hoss, steady. So-ho there!

JEWISH GENTLEMAN

Hey, you! Take those damned camels where my horse can't wind 'em! *(He dashes out (R.B.).)*

MERCHANT *(down, left)*

Taxes! that's what it means, more taxes! Why else should they take a census? Just idle curiosity on the part of the Imperial Government?

GREEK GENTLEMAN

Well, sir, I imagine they must find occupation for the staff at the Home Office. Besides, the Emperor takes a great interest in vital statistics.

MERCHANT

Vital statistics my foot! They mean to clap on a poll-tax, you see if they don't. As if we weren't squeezed and badgered enough already, what with Imperial taxes and the King's taxes, customs, excise, land-tax, house-tax, and now this monstrous new stamp-duty on sales. Trade, sir, trade is the life-blood of the country, and they're strangling it, deliberately doing all they can to strangle it, with these iniquitous exactions. But there! I can tell by your speech you're a foreigner. Perhaps they manage things better where you come from. *(Sits on HUSBAND'S baggage, left.)*

GREEK GENTLEMAN

I am a Greek, sir; Philip is my name. I am travelling to
Jerusalem with letters of introduction to the King's his-
torian. I dabble a little in letters—oh, very amateurishly,
I assure you—and have foolishly undertaken to write a
trifling study of social and economic conditions in the
Roman provinces. Anything I can learn about the effect of
legislation on commerce is of great assistance to my ignorance.

{LANDLORD *re-enters right (R.U.) and checks papers with*
CENTURION; *they move up back.*}

MERCHANT

Well, you can put it in your book, sir, that the effect of this
kind of legislation is disastrous. I don't mince words, I say
disastrous. Between the King and the Emperor, we're
between the upper and the nether millstones. The King
pampers the labouring classes at the expense of respectable
citizens, and the Emperor makes it his business to thrust a
crowbar into the wheels at every opportunity. . . .

HUSBAND

Confound you, sir, that's my bag you're sitting on. *(He jerks
his luggage away and returns up left.)*

MERCHANT

. . . It's a scandal to disturb honest tradesmen at the busiest
time of the year, and send them trapesing up and down the
country, just to get themselves registered at some infernal
village where they had the misfortune to be born. Here's
weeks of valuable time wasted—not to mention the peril to
life and limb.

{LANDLADY *works up and off, left (L.U.).*}

GREEK GENTLEMAN

Certainly the roads are in a shocking state—and terribly
congested.

{JEWISH GENTLEMAN *comes out of stable (L.B.) and goes in
again (R.B.).*}

MERCHANT

Congested? That's nothing. They're not safe, my good sir,
they're not safe! Bandits and revolutionaries lurking in every
thicket. My heart was in my mouth all the way, and we
passed some most ruffianly-looking characters in the hill-
country near Beth-Horon. I suppose, by the way, you don't
know anybody who's travelling back in that direction, and
would permit me to join his company?

GREEK GENTLEMAN

I'm afraid not. I'm a stranger here myself, you know. But
we might ask the Roman centurion over there. He seems to
be checking up on the arrivals.

MERCHANT

Thank you, thank you, that's an excellent suggestion. Will
you add to your kindness by accompanying me? I don't like
the look of some of these people—I'm sure they'd pick your
purse as soon as look at you. *(They move up centre. To* WIFE)
Excuse me, madam, I wish to speak to the Centurion. *(To*
HUSBAND) Allow me, sir. *(They grudgingly make way for him.)*
This place is dreadfully overcrowded. *(He encounters* MAN-
SERVANT *and* FATHER, *returning from the stable, their shoulders
laden with a pack-saddle, goatskins, cooking utensils, etc.)* Pray let
me pass, my good fellows. *(They shove past him, thrusting him
aside upon the* BOY, *who utters a sharp yell.)* Oh, I beg your
pardon, I didn't see your little boy; I hope I've not hurt him.

MOTHER *(venomously)*

Some people want all the place to themselves!
   {*In the meantime, the* CENTURION *has moved across with the*
   LANDLORD *to the left upper corner of the stage, and is as far off as
   ever. The* MERCHANT, *with a despairing cry, darts after him in
   this new direction, and becomes involved with the* LANDLADY *and
   the* MAIDSERVANT, *who enter left (L.U.), bringing some cooked
   food to the* HUSBAND *and* WIFE.}

MERCHANT

Dear, dear, I'm sorry. How clumsy of me! Pardon, pardon.

144

LANDLADY *(looking daggers)*

Granted, I'm sure.
{*The* CENTURION *and* LANDLORD *come halfway down by passage, left; the* MERCHANT *following. The* GREEK GENTLE-MAN, *smiling imperturbably, insinuates himself neatly through the crowd in the* MERCHANT'S *wake, and everybody thinks him charming.*}

MERCHANT *(arriving at last)*

Good evening, Captain. Can you spare me just a moment of your time?

CENTURION

In one minute, sir. Here, landlord, all these papers seem to be in order. I shouldn't think there'd be any more arrivals now. You'd better close the gates.

LANDLORD

Yes, Captain. Thank you, Captain. I don't see how we could take anybody else if they did come *(Shouting.)* Porter, bar the gates!

PORTER *(shouting off, right)*

There's another party here wants to come in.

LANDLORD

What's that?

PORTER

There's a party here with a donkey. I've told 'em there ain't no room.

LANDLORD

All right, I'll come myself. *(He comes down left and starts to cross behind* PHARISEE, *turning as he goes to speak to the* CENTURION.) There wasn't anything further, was there, Captain?

145

CENTURION

> No, that's all right. Carry on.
> {*Exit* LANDLORD, *right.*}
> Now, Master Merchant, what can I do for you?

MERCHANT

> I was wondering, Captain, whether you knew of anyone
> who would be returning by way of Beth-Horon?

CENTURION

> Well, let me see, now. Why, yes, there's a young gentleman
> going through that way to-morrow as far as Lydda. I forget
> his name, but you'll find him somewhere about, wearing a
> Roman dress and a green cloak.

MERCHANT

> Thank you, Captain, thank you. I am going to Lydda
> myself.
> > {*Re-enter, right,* LANDLORD. *He backs in, making expostulatory*
> > *gestures.* JOSEPH *follows, pleading with him.* MARY *comes quietly*
> > *behind* JOSEPH.}
> Is he a wealthy gentleman, with plenty of armed servants?
> Do you think he would permit me to join his party?

LANDLORD

> No, no, no, I tell you.

JOSEPH

> Yes, but do listen a moment . . .
> > {LANDLADY *works across to them.*}

CENTURION (*to* MERCHANT)

> Couldn't say, I'm sure, sir. You'd better ask him. (*His eye has*
> *been caught by the little disturbance on the other side of the stage.*)
> Excuse me, the landlord seems to be having a spot of bother
> over there. I'll have to go and keep an eye on it. Now then,
> good people, out of my way, please! (*He strides uncere-*
> *moniously across the centre of the stage.*)

146

MANSERVANT *(obsequiously)*

Clear the way for the Captain!

MOTHER *(snatching her Boy out of the way)*

Look out, here's the Centurion coming.

FATHER *(finding himself accidentally blocking the CENTURION'S path and being unceremoniously shoved aside)*

Beg your pardon, Captain. *(Aside.)* Damn your Roman insolence!

CENTURION *(whisking round)*

Hey?

FATHER

Nothing, Captain.
{*Meanwhile the MERCHANT and the GREEK GENTLEMAN have wandered off left to look for the JEWISH GENTLEMAN.*}

LANDLORD

I'm sorry, my good man, I tell you it's absolutely impossible.

JOSEPH

I implore you, good host, in the name of all the Prophets . . .

LANDLORD

Be reasonable, man. I don't mean it unkindly. It can't be done, that's all. We're packed right out—aren't we, wife?

LANDLADY

Packed out? I should think we were. I'm sure I don't know how we shall manage as it is. Not an inch of space down here, as you can see for yourselves, and they're sleeping on the roof head to tail like herrings in a basket. Indecent, I call it. The Government's got no right to land poor inkeepers in such a pickle.

CENTURION

Now then, ma'am. What's the trouble here?

JOSEPH

Good soldier, can you help us to find a lodging for the night? We have sought everywhere in the town, and this is our last hope.

LANDLORD

And I'm telling him, Captain, we haven't so much as a corner. They'll have to push on to Jerusalem.

LANDLADY

It's only five miles, and it's a big place.

JOSEPH

Alas! sir, it's very late and a bad road. Will you not persuade this worthy couple to give us a shake-down somewhere? We are not particular. As you see, we are humble folk, and there are only the two of us.

LANDLADY

Yes, and like to be three of you before long, I reckon.

JOSEPH

Indeed, that's true. My wife is in no fit state to travel farther. Besides, our journey ends here.

LANDLORD

Captain, you can see we are not to blame——

CENTURION

Wait a bit, wait a bit. Let's get this straight. You, good master, what's your name?

JOSEPH

I am called Joseph ben Heli, and this is Mary, my wife.

CENTURION

Trade?

JOSEPH

Carpenter.

CENTURION

Place of residence?

JOSEPH

Nazareth in Galilee.

CENTURION

Lineage?

JOSEPH

Of the house and lineage of David.

CENTURION

Of David, eh? And this is the city of David?

JOSEPH

Yes, Captain.

CENTURION

And therefore the proper place for you to get yourselves registered?

JOSEPH

Yes, Captain.

CENTURION

I see. Well, it does seem a bit hard to move you on, especially as your good lady is so near her time. What do you say, landlord? Can't you shift some of the baggage and give them shelter under the arches?

{*During the following conversation, MANSERVANT and MAID-SERVANT bring in three braziers, placing one for the MOTHER, who uses it to cook supper, one just below the HUSBAND and WIFE, and the third near the PHARISEE.*}

LANDLORD

Don't see how we can, sir. We've got all the servants of these ladies and gentlemen bedded down there as it is. You couldn't put a pin between 'em. It's not my fault if people will travel with such a lot of attendants. Inconsiderate, I call it, but there you are.

CENTURION

How about the stables? Is there any room there?

LANDLORD

Well, I dunno about that. Let me see now—it means getting their ass in as well. Could you lie along of the ass, mistress?

MARY

Yes, indeed we could. She's a quiet good creature and gives no trouble, does she, Joseph?

JOSEPH

None whatever. Thank you kindly. A stable would be far better than nothing.

LANDLORD

I haven't promised anything yet. Let me put on my thinking cap. We can't move the camels, nor yet put the young gentleman's stallion in with the mares. Perhaps we could—— No! that won't work.

LANDLADY

Could we make room for the captain's gelding along of the merchant's she-asses—if you didn't mind, sir—

150

CENTURION

Not in the least. By all means.

LANDLORD

That's a good idea. Then we could put these people and their donkey in with old Ibrahim's draught-ox. How would that suit you?

JOSEPH

Excellently. We are greatly obliged to you.

MARY

It is most kind of you. We are sorry to be putting you to all this extra trouble on our account.

LANDLORD

That's all right. Don't like to think of you with nowhere to lay your heads. Especially under the circumstances, eh, wife?

LANDLADY

It's not that anybody *wants* to seem disobliging——

CENTURION

Of course not, of course not. Well, that's all settled. I'm sure you'll manage capitally. Good night to you. (*He joins the* SOLDIERS *and confers with them.*)

MARY *and* JOSEPH

Good night, Captain.
    {*Here the* MERCHANT *reappears, left (L.U.), followed by the* GREEK GENTLEMAN. *They move along the passage-way at the back.*}

LANDLORD

Now you come along with me. I'll have some clean straw put down for you. (*Calling off right.*) Take the ass round to

the stable! *(Hoofs heard off right and round to centre back.)* Mind
how you go; you'll have to pick your way a bit. *(They move
up back and across among the piled-up baggage in the passage-way.)*
It's just across here and under the—
   {*The MERCHANT falls over a pack-saddle, into the LANDLORD'S
   arms.*}
Ouf! you might look where you're going, sir!

MERCHANT *(panting)*

I'm extremely sorry, Landlord. Could you tell me . . . Oh,
dear! *(He is out of breath.)*

GREEK GENTLEMAN

Landlord, we are looking for a young gentleman in a green
cloak. Have you by any chance seen such a one?
   {*JEWISH GENTLEMAN emerges from stable, R.B.*}

LANDLORD

This'll be him, sir, just coming through the archway.

MERCHANT

Oh, thank you, thank you!

LANDLORD

Don't mention it. *(He enters the centre stable with MARY and
JOSEPH.)*
   {*LANDLADY has meanwhile worked away left.*}

MERCHANT

Sir! Pray, one moment, young gentleman!

JEWISH GENTLEMAN

Hullo!

GREEK GENTLEMAN

Your pardon, sir. This good merchant wishes to ask you—
(with a change of tone) Now, by all the gods of Olympus! If it
isn't my old friend Yussuf!

JEWISH GENTLEMAN

Philip! by all the Prophets! What on earth are you doing
here? *(They come down right.)*

GREEK GENTLEMAN

Just travelling about. Studying social history and all that.
Writing a little verse, and tinkering about with a magnum
opus that will never get finished.

JEWISH GENTLEMAN

The same old Philip. Not changed a bit since college days.
I'm delighted to see you. Come and sit down and let's have
a yarn.

MERCHANT *(panting after them)*

Forgive me, sir, but I——

GREEK GENTLEMAN

Oh, yes, I forgot. This honest merchant wants to know if he
may have the protection of your company as far as Lydda.
*{Meanwhile LANDLORD may be seen taking straw in to stable,
C.B.; MAIDSERVANT may take in water, etc., and fasten curtain
of sacking across entrance.}*

JEWISH GENTLEMAN

Certainly, by all means. The more the merrier. I hope, sir,
you'll join us in a cup of wine.

MERCHANT

I am very much obliged, sir.

JEWISH GENTLEMAN

Here's a good place to sit in, near this worthy Pharisee.
(They all sit by PHARISEE.) I trust we do not disturb you, sir.
Thank you. Shockingly crowded this place is to-night, and
I entirely agree with you, merchant, that travelling's no
joke these days.

MERCHANT

Terrible, sir, terrible! Times are hard enough, goodness
knows, without Caesar taking it into his head to number
the people. Apart from everything else, look at the inter-
ruption to business. It's a sin and a shame——

PHARISEE (interrupting)

It is a sin indeed to number the people. It is the sin
of King David, to which Satan provoked him. Is it not
written in the Book of the Chronicles of the Kings of Israel?

GREEK GENTLEMAN

I have not studied the work in question, but I'll take your
word for it.

JEWISH GENTLEMAN

You may take his word for it, Philip. He is a learned
Pharisee, and he ought to know.

PHARISEE

Judging by your dress, gentlemen, and by the speech of one
of you, you are Romans.

JEWISH GENTLEMAN

My friend is Greek, but I am as good a Jew as yourself, sir.
I was educated in Rome, certainly, and prefer to dress in
the fashion.

PHARISEE

God deliver us from the fashions of Rome—where they
teach our Hebrew youth to sneer at God's word and bind a
foreign yoke and a pagan custom upon our necks in flat
defiance of the Law of Moses.
    {Throughout this conversation, the LANDLORD, LANDLADY, and
    SERVANTS move unobtrusively about, looking after the travellers,
    who eat their supper and prepare for the night. Some of this action
    can be supposed to take place off, left, in attendance on people

upstairs; and the MANSERVANT *can go in and out of the stables. The* CENTURION *goes centre and stands behind the brazier warm-int his hands.*}

JEWISH GENTLEMAN

Nonsense, sir! Surely one can be a sincere Jew and still live like a gentleman?

PHARISEE *(contemptuously)*

Like a gentleman!

JEWISH GENTLEMAN

Yes, sir. I come of a good house; my father is a magistrate. I shall probably end up as a member of the Sanhedrim myself when the time comes. And when I'm there, be sure I shall press for a more enlightened and cosmopolitan policy.

PHARISEE

Indeed, sir! Well, I am Zadok the Pharisee, a follower of Judas the Gaulonite, and I say that your godless Roman-ising policy is bringing upon this nation the curse due to the backslider and the apostate.

JEWISH GENTLEMAN

Upon my soul, sir——!
   {*This little passage of arms attracts the attention of the* CEN-TURION. *Seeing that it quiets down, he takes no action, but he keeps his eye on it.*}

MERCHANT

Pray, gentlemen, don't quarrel. I'm a man of peace. I quite see your point, good Master Zadok. You're bound to look at things from the religious side. But I'm a plain man, and what I object to is the inconvenience. Here I am, torn from my home, put in peril of my life, and goodness knows what's happening to my business all this time! That scoundrelly Greek—Oh, I beg your pardon, noble sir—that manager of

155

mine is probably making hay of the accounts, and I shall lose all my best customers. I'm a spice-merchant, gentleme, Aaron ben Isaac is my name, in a pretty big way down at Joppa.

PHARISEE

I'm glad you stick to the old-fashioned native name.

MERCHANT

Did I say Joppa? I meant Caesarea, of course. Caesarea we call it now, since Herod rebuilt it and made all those modern improvements. A heathen name, of course, but what's in a name?—and I must say, the King has succeeded in putting the town on the map. Here's my card, by the way, if you should happen to be requiring pepper, or perfumes, or anything in that line. I have the honour to supply nutmegs to the Imperial Household.

{The LANDLORD, with a jug of wine in his hand, is now centre of stage. He serves HUSBAND and prepares to go off left.}

JEWISH GENTLEMAN

Thanks very much. I'd be glad to know of any one who can supply bath-unguents and toilet-waters reasonably. The prices in Jerusalem are positively outrageous. Landlord! bring us some wine here!

{LANDLORD returns with a jar of wine.}

PHARISEE

Bath-unguents, indeed! That's all you young men think about. It was a black day for Jewry when King Herod built the public baths for the corruption of our young men.

{The CENTURION, smelling trouble, wanders casually up to the back of the group, with the detached air of a London policeman patrolling a public meeting.}

You loll about there all day, oiling your bodies and anointing your hair, reading lascivious heathen poetry, talking blasphemy, and idling away the time with Greek slaves and dancing-girls. May the curse of Korah, Dathan, and Abiram light on King Herod and his baths too! May the earth open and swallow them up!

156

LANDLORD

> Your wine, gentlemen. *(Whispering.)* Sir, I implore you not
> to talk so loudly. King Herod's spies are everywhere. And
> the centurion is standing just behind you.

JEWISH GENTLEMAN

> Serve to the gentlemen. Your health, sirs. Personally I'm all
> for King Herod. He may be a bit of an autocrat, but he's
> done a lot for the country. How about his big housing
> schemes in Samaria, and Caesarea with its great new har-
> bour and up-to-date drainage system?

MERCHANT

> That's a fact. You wouldn't know the old place.

GREEK GENTLEMAN

> I must make a point of visiting it.

JEWISH GENTLEMAN

> Look at the Jordan Valley Waterworks. Look at the Temple
> in Jerusalem. Look at the theatres and amphitheatres the
> King has built and endowed——

PHARISEE

> Nothing would induce me to look at them. Play-acting and
> wild-beast shows are an abomination in the sight of the
> Lord. Immoral, irreligious, and thoroughly un-Jewish.

JEWISH GENTLEMAN

> Yes, they *are* un-Jewish. Our national attitude to the Arts is
> deplorable. King Herod is the only Jew in the country who
> cares twopence about cosmopolitan culture.

PHARISEE

> Thank God for it. Nothing is so demoralising as art and cul-
> ture. As for Herod, he is no true Israelite. He is an Edomite,
> a son of Ishmael, and, what's more, an unbeliever. He

breaks the Law of Moses by letting the barbarians in the provinces put up graven images to him. And you, Aaron ben Isaac, who complain of the Imperial taxes, have you forgotten that it is unlawful to pay tribute to Caesar?

{*The* CENTURION *at this point really does take notice.*}

LANDLORD

Hush, hush, sir, for Heaven's sake!

MERCHANT (*alarmed*)

Here, I say! Hadn't you better be careful?

PHARISEE

You have no spirit. You are slaves, sold by Herod into the bondage of Rome—and all you can do is to sit there grumbling feebly about taxation and interruptions to business. What room will there be for such as you in the great day of redemption when the Lord's Messiah comes?

CENTURION

And what will your Messiah do when he does come?

LANDLORD

God of Abraham! I knew there'd be trouble. I'm sure, Captain, the gentleman means no harm. Don't hold it against me. This is a respectable house.

MERCHANT

Of course, of course, Captain. And anyway, I wasn't saying anything. I swear I haven't uttered a syllable against the Emperor or King Herod either. I never suggested the taxes were illegal. I only said they came heavy on a man, and so they do—but there's nothing treasonable in that.

JEWISH GENTLEMAN

That's what taxes are for—to give us something to grumble about. Eh, Captain? Sit down, man, and have a drink.

GREEK GENTLEMAN

That's right, Captain. Fill for the Captain, landlord.

CENTURION

Thank you kindly, sir. I don't mind if I do. Cheer up, landlord, we're not going to crucify you yet awhile.

LANDLORD *(pouring wine for CENTURION)*

No, sir. Thank you, sir. *(He retires, left.)*
{*Sound of singing and marching off, back.*}

CENTURION

Your health, sir! The gods be favourable to you. Cheer up, Master Merchant. So long as the taxes are paid, Rome can put up with a grumble or two.

MERCHANT *(with a wry face)*

Yes, yes, of course——

CENTURION

And, after all, we do give you something to show for the money.

PHARISEE *(sarcastically)*

Undoubtedly. Baths and theatres and drainage systems, and other worldly luxuries that our fathers did very well without.

CENTURION

Better than that, sir. Peace and security. Listen!

SONG OF THE LEGIONAIRES *(as they pass the inn)*

> Bread and cheese, bread and cheese
> Marching through Spain, boys,
> With a sackful of loot
> And a hole in your boot
> At the end of the long campaign, boys;
> Bread and cheese, bread and cheese.

159

{*The* ROMAN SOLDIERS *join in for a bar or two.*}
                    Early and late, boys,
                    For we'll get no cheer
                    Of beef and beer
                    Till we see the Julian gate, boys.
                    Beef and beer, beef and beer, etc., etc.
{*The song dies away off right, past the gate.*}

CENTURION

Those are the lads of the Sixth, going up to keep order in
Jerusalem. Good luck to 'em. And to King Herod too, say I.
Regular good army man, is King Herod.
  {*The* MERCHANT *endorses these sentiments with eager nods.*}
Judaea was in a pretty mess till he took it over. He and the
Emperor together have kept order these thirty years. No
invasions, no civil wars, peace and prosperity and a reason-
able check kept on bandits and insurgents. What more do
you want?

PHARISEE *(with dignity)*

Peace is not everything. Prosperity is not everything. *(The*
MERCHANT *tugs anxiously at his sleeve, but he continues.)* We
want liberty for our nation and liberty for our religion.

CENTURION

Bless my heart, what do you think liberty means? Liberty to
cut one another's throats—as you were doing before Rome
stepped in and put a stop to it? There's no liberty in civil dis-
order. Liberty means freedom to go safely about your business and behave yourselves like good citizens. And you'll
only get that under a strong central government. Do you
think your Christ or Messiah or whatever you call him is
going to beat Rome at that game?

PHARISEE

When the Messiah comes——

JEWISH GENTLEMAN

Need we argue about the Messiah?

MERCHANT

No, no, of course not. Let's keep clear of politics.

GREEK GENTLEMAN

Yes, but what is the Messiah?

PHARISEE

When the Messiah comes, he will restore the kingdom to
Israel and smite the heathen with a rod of iron.
    {MERCHANT groans.}

CENTURION

I can't understand you Jews. Can't you live and let live?
Nobody minds your worshipping what you please and how
you please. The Emperor's very keen on religious toleration.
We've got temples in Rome to all sorts of odd foreign deities,
you'd be surprised; and if you liked to put one up there to
your Jehovah, or whatever you call him, there's no reason
why he and our Jove shouldn't get on capitally together.

PHARISEE

The Lord God of Heaven is One God and One alone. We
can make no compromise with idols.

CENTURION

It seems to me you want all the religious liberty for yourselves and none for other people. Well, it's no affair of
mine. But if your Messiah is proposing to start a war of
religion——

MERCHANT

Really, now, really. Do let's leave the Messiah out of it. So
far as I know, he isn't even born yet.

CENTURION

Very sensible of him. If he takes my advice he'll put off
being born for quite a little bit. King Herod has done a very

tidy job keeping order in this province and he has no use at all for Messiahs and insurrections. Good evening. *(He marches off left, and is seen to speak to the LANDLORD, who follows him off.)*

{LEGIONAIRES *heard again, singing: "Beef and beer."*}

MERCHANT

Heaven preserve us! my heart was in my mouth. All this treasonable talk——

JEWISH GENTLEMAN

Zadok, do you never think that this stiff-necked resistance may end by destroying our nation?

PHARISEE

Your easy toleration will end by destroying our souls. How long, O Lord, how long? *(He stalks stiffly away, and settles down left.)*

SONG OF THE LEGIONAIRES

{*As the LANDLADY passes on some errand, the* 1st SOLDIER *puts his arm round her. She pushes him off. Laughter.*}
Beef and beer, beef and beer
Sitting at home, sweet home, boys,
With a wench in your arm
To keep you warm,
O take me back to Rome, boys!

MERCHANT

Men like that are a public danger.
{*Knocking off, right, and sounds of argument with the* PORTER.}
Oh, dear me! Are the soldiers coming in? Bear witness, gentlemen, I never saw him before.
{LANDLADY *extricates herself from the* SOLDIERS *and hurries off, right.* MERCHANT *retires to remote corner down left, below* PHARISEE.}

SONG (continued)

> Beef and beer, beef and beer,
> And cram your bellies tight, boys,
> For it's starve and freeze
> On bread and cheese
> When the eagles take their flight, boys.
> Bread and cheese, bread and cheese, etc.

LANDLADY (shrilly; backing in, right)

Now then, now then, what do you want at this time of night?
It's no good, I tell you, my man. We're full up. Can't take
anybody else. You needn't start arguing. We're full up.

1ST SHEPHERD

Excuse me, ma'am. My mate and me only looked in to see
if we could buy a drop o' beer.

LANDLADY

Beer? Good gracious me, what next? This is an inn for
travellers, not a jug-and-bottle department. You must go to
the wine-shop in the next street.
  {SHEPHERDS edge in after her.}

1ST SHEPHERD

The wine-shop's shut, ma'am, and we thought if you'd be
so good as to oblige us——

LANDLADY

Nonsense. You must knock the wine-merchant up—or go
without, much better for you. Get along now and don't
hang about the doorway. You smell of the sheepfolds. Be off
with you!

JEWISH GENTLEMAN (calling up-stage)

Oh, for Heaven's sake, woman, stop screaming!

LANDLADY

Oh, dear! That's the young gentleman from Rome. Now
he'll be vexed. *(Coming down.)* I'm sure I'm very sorry, sir;
it's these common shepherds, pushing in here, wanting to
buy beer, as if this was a vulgar alehouse. I've told them as
plain as I could——

JEWISH GENTLEMAN

I heard you. Your voice, sweet hostess, goes through my
head like a knife through a melon. Can't you give these
honest lads their beer and have done with it?
    {SHEPHERDS *advance hopefully.*}

LANDLADY

We don't sell beer.

JEWISH GENTLEMAN

You grasp the idea, lads, don't you? We don't sell beer
What are you? Shepherds?

1ST SHEPHERD

Yes, sir. We weren't wishful to be troublesome. Me and my
two sons be keepin' our sheep on the hills yonder, and, it
bein' a cold sort o' night, Sam and me come along to get a
little drop to our supper.

JEWISH GENTLEMAN

I see. Well, I haven't got any beer, but here's wine, if that'll
suit you. Sit down and have a quick one before you go.

1ST *and* 2ND SHEPHERDS

Thank you, sir. Very good of you, sir.
    {*They gather about the* JEWISH GENTLEMAN—*he gives them
    wine.*}

164

JEWISH GENTLEMAN

All right, hostess, that will do. *(Exit LANDLADY, working off, left (L.U.).)* Now, tell me, my good friends, how are things going with you? Do you rub along pretty well? Or do you want a rebellion against the Government, and a new Messiah and all that kind of thing? You can talk quite freely to us. We shan't give you away. My friend here is studying social conditions, aren't you, Phil?

GREEK GENTLEMAN

Yes; I am very much interested in your Jewish religion and politics; but they are terribly complicated. This, for instance, your Messiah as you call him—what does that word mean, Yussuf?

JEWISH GENTLEMAN

Christos in Greek, Christ, the Anointed One.
{*During this long conversation, the rest of the travellers settle down to sleep. The 1ST SOLDIER stands sentinel at the door, right; the other goes to sleep. The lights in the other two braziers die down, leaving only the group of the two GENTLEMEN and the SHEPHERDS clearly lit, and a beam of moonlight on the stable door. Dim down front spots and No. 3 batten gradually.*}

GREEK GENTLEMAN

Ah, yes. Messiah, Christ, I understand. Now, this anointed one—what is he? A king or a priest? Or is he some kind of hero or demi-god, after the fashion of our Hercules?

JEWISH GENTLEMAN

My dear man, these shepherds have never heard of Hercules.

GREEK GENTLEMAN

Never mind. I like to get the reactions of the common people to all these academic questions. What do you think of Christ, my good friends?

1ST SHEPHERD

Well, sir, I don't rightly know. Some say he's to be a great
prince, born of the royal house of David—him that was a
king in Israel, you know, sir, long ago, wonderful rich and
powerful, notwithstanding he began life as a poor shepherd,
no better than us. But others say he'll be a mighty chieftain,
more after the style of Judas the Maccabean, and lead a
great rebellion against Rome. But I do hope and trust it
won't be that way, sir—not in our time, anyway.

JEWISH GENTLEMAN

You don't want a rebellion, then?

1ST SHEPHERD

That I do not, sir. Rebellions and civil wars and such never
do no good to us poor folk.

2ND SHEPHERD

Come now, Father, I don't know. They say the Messiah will
restore the kingdom and do away with oppression and taxes,
and bring back the good old days, with milk and honey for
everybody.
{About this point, JOESPH comes out of stable door (C.B.). He
quietly wakes the MAIDSERVANT, who goes off left (L.U.), to
look for LANDLADY. JOSEPH returns to stable.}

1ST SHEPHERD

Why, so he may; but there'll be a sight of poor souls ruined
and slaughtered first. No; life's hard enough on the poor, as
it is, without no wars. We're well enough off as we are, with
King Herod. You'll find, sir, it's mostly the upper classes as
complains about King Herod's government. He don't bear
too hard on the farmers, all things considered. Of course
some of the tax-gatherers put the screw on cruel, but,
saving your presence, gentlemen, I think they mostly gets
their orders from the Emperor, and him living 'way off in
Rome, maybe he don't quite know how the way they go on here.

2ND SHEPHERD

Maybe, when Messiah comes, he'll explain matters to the
Emperor. You know, sirs, there's some say he won't be a
king at all—but a poor, good man, the servant of the people.
Something more in the nature of a prophet, like, same as
Elias, or it might be Nathan, what spoke and rebuked King
David when he behaved so unjust to Uriah the Hittite.
{Enter LANDLADY, left (L.U.), with lantern. She goes briskly
in at stable door (C.B.).}

1ST SHEPHERD

Yes, or a holy priest, more after the fashion of Aaron or
Melchisedek, as will take away sin and bring the people
back to righteousness—for there's a sad deal of worldly
living these days, and men don't keep the Law as they did.
Some of the young people don't seem to believe in nothing
but dancing and going to prize-fights and having a good
time.

2nd SHEPHERD

That's right. And there's a young chap I know, that's
employed in the theatre, as they call it, at Jerusalem, says
the goings-on there is something shocking—men dressed up
like women with masks on, acting heathen pieces full of smut
and nastiness, and tumblers and chariot-races, and a terrible
deal of betting and gambling. It ain't right, to our way of
thinking. I expect Messiah will put a stop to all that.
{The CENTURION reappears, left, and passes silently across the
back of the stage, the moonlight catching his helmet as he goes past
the stable. He goes out, right.}

1ST SHEPHERD

Ay, so he will, I dare say. But he won't do it by making wars.
People don't act holier in war-time, they acts more sinful.
And what with soldiers stravaguing up and down, looting
and pillaging and destroying the cattle and the crops, it's a
bad business for everyone. No, we don't want no more wars.

GREEK GENTLEMAN

Upon my word, Yussuf, your countrymen seem to be very
sensible fellows. Here's to you, shepherds, and I hope, when
your Messiah comes, he'll turn out to be a prince of peace.
If you ask my opinion——
{LANDLADY *comes briskly out of stable door, with* JOSEPH
following.}

LANDLADY

There now, didn't I tell you so?

JEWISH GENTLEMAN

Hullo! what's the matter with our good hostess now?

LANDLADY

It's no good talking that way to me, Joseph ben Heli; this is
an inn, not a lying-in hospital. Of all the tiresome things!
No, indeed I can't help you—I've got far too much to do.
Perhaps there's some one among the company that can
oblige. Excuse me, ladies, is there anybody here that's a
midwife?

FATHER

Eh, what? Yes, my missus is a very good hand in that line.
Wake up, Hepzibah, you're wanted.
{MOTHER *gets up.*}

MOTHER

What is it? (FATHER *whispers.*) Oh, yes, of course.

LANDLADY

Very good of you, I'm sure. I wouldn't have had this
happen for the world. It all comes of being soft-hearted and
letting people in against one's better judgment. She's in the
stable over there, in the far corner—you'll know it by the
brown ox being there. Here, take this lantern.

JOSEPH

I'll carry the lantern to light the kind midwife.

LANDLADY

Indeed, my good man, you'll do no such thing. We don't
want any husbands hanging around. This is a woman's job.
Oh, dear! oh, dear! we shall none of us get any sleep to-
night. And I don't suppose for one moment you thought to
bring any proper swaddling-clothes with you.

JOSEPH

Yes, ma'am, indeed we came provided. The midwife will
find everything needful in our saddle-bags.
{MOTHER *disappears into stable. The family group settles down
again.*}

LANDLADY

Well, that's a mercy. Bless me, what an upset!

JEWISH GENTLEMAN

Sweet mistress, do I gather we're expecting an addition to
the company?

LANDLADY

Yes, indeed, sir, and I'm sure I'm very sorry for all this dis-
turbance. It's this man's wife been taken with her pains, sir,
and I really don't wonder, riding up all the way from
Nazareth, and over these bad roads. It's a wicked thing, sir,
isn't it, that decent folk should be jostled about and sent
travelling willy-nilly, just because the Government takes it
into its head to have a census.

1ST SHEPHERD

Ah! it's a shame, that it is.

JEWISH GENTLEMAN

Very trying indeed.

169

LANDLADY

We had to bed them down in the stable—along with the ox
and the ass—and where we're to put the child, I really don't
know. There isn't a cradle in the place. I had one, but I gave
it to my daughter when she married. You'll have to use the
manger, that's all. I'll go and find you some old sacking to
line it with.

JOSEPH

God will reward you for all your kindness.

LANDLADY

Oh, well, it's all in the day's work, I suppose.
{*Exit* LANDLADY, *left (L.U.).*}

1ST SHEPHERD

We'd better be getting along to the sheep now. Thank you
kindly for the wine, sir. Good luck to you, Master Carpenter. May your good lady have a light childbirth.

2ND SHEPHERD

Ay, truly, and bring you a bonny baby to bless you.

JOSEPH

I thank you both from my heart.
{*Exeunt* SHEPHERDS, *right. Gate is noisily barred after them.*}

JEWISH GENTLEMAN

Take courage, good man. These things happen every day.
It's sure to be all right. Here, I'll have a wager with you.
What odds will you lay me it's a boy?

JOSEPH

It would be robbing you, young sir. I know it will be a boy.

GREEK GENTLEMAN

Hark at him! Every father is certain it will be a boy.

JEWISH GENTLEMAN

And every Jewish mother is certain it will be the Messiah. Isn't that so, carpenter?

JOSEPH

That is so.

JEWISH GENTLEMAN

And what are you going to call your Messiah when you get him?

JOSEPH

His name shall be called Jesus; for he was so named of an angel before he was conceived in the womb.

GREEK GENTLEMAN

Jesus? and what does that mean?

JEWISH GENTLEMAN

Oh, it's quite a common Jewish name. It means liberator, a deliverer, a savior—that sort of thing.

JOSEPH

He is to be called Jesus, because he shall save his people from their sins. The angel said so to his mother.

GREEK GENTLEMAN

He seems to have been a very communicative and explicit angel. What else did he say to your wife?

JOSEPH

He said, "The Holy Ghost shall come upon thee and the power of the most High shall overshadow thee; therefore that holy thing that shall be born of thee shall be called the Son of God."

GREEK GENTLEMAN

> The son of a god. The expression seems very familiar. Our Greek mythology is full of such tales. Personally, I am an agnostic, but I am always willing to learn. Pray tell me, carpenter, did the god manifest himself in a shower of gold, as Jupiter did to Danae?

JEWISH GENTLEMAN

> Be quiet, Philip. The God of Israel is nothing like your heathen deities. He is a spirit, and works, not after the flesh, but after the spirit. Besides, your own philosophers will tell you that your Olympic myths are themselves no more than symbols of the working of the spirit upon the flesh.

GREEK GENTLEMAN

> So they say, indeed. But I believe the whole thing is nothing but a pack of fairy-tales.

JEWISH GENTLEMAN

> I don't know, Philip. Sometimes I have wondered whether the Son of God, when He comes, might not fulfil your prophecies as well as ours. The hearts of all men have felt obscurely that God should somehow reveal Himself—walk as a man with men—I do not know. Does not Aeschylus speak somewhere of a Zeus that should know human suffering?

GREEK GENTLEMAN

> Yes; in the *Eumenides*. But I thought your God was rather an exclusive deity, and never troubled Himself about any but His chosen people.

JEWISH GENTLEMAN

> I know. But we insist very loudly that He is God of the whole earth. One would expect Him to take some interest in the outlying portions of His dominions. What do you say, carpenter?
>
> {PHARISEE *gets up and comes across, right.*}

172

JOSEPH

I do not know at all, sir. I am a plain ignorant man. I try
only to do my duty and obey the word of God without
asking too many questions. But here is a Pharisee coming
across to us. He is no doubt learned in the Scriptures.
Perhaps he can tell us.

JEWISH GENTLEMAN

Why, if it isn't my old friend Zadok. You seem to be restless,
sir. I hope our talk hasn't disturbed you.

PHARISEE (with more concession to common humanity than
he has shown up till now)

The snoring of Aaron ben Isaac the merchant is a curse
more intolerable than all the ten plagues of Egypt. The
bellowing of fat bulls of Bashan is silence by comparison.

GREEK GENTLEMAN

You have come in time to settle a theological argument. My
friend here says that the God of Israel is lord of the whole
earth, and in consequence the Messiah will be the saviour of
the Gentiles as well as of the Jews. Do you support that
opinion.

PHARISEE

Certainly not. It is blasphemous and ridiculous. He will set
his foot upon the necks of the nations, and the heathen will
be cast into outer darkness with wailing and gnashing of
teeth. I hope you are answered. This inn seems to be very
noisy to-night. I am going outside to try and get a little
peace and quietness. (He goes out by door to stair, left (L.U.),
passing LANDLADY, who goes into stable (C.B.).)

GREEK GENTLEMAN

What a very dogmatic person! It must be marvellous to feel
so positive about everything. I never feel certain of anything.

JEWISH GENTLEMAN

That is the malady of you Greeks—you are blown about
with every wind. Ours is to shut ourselves up tight in
tradition and exclude every breath of fresh air. If only we
could somehow wed the purity of our religion to the intellectual vigour of your philosophy! Well, never mind. Sing
to us, Philip, and take our minds off our worries.

GREEK GENTLEMAN

Will it not disturb the company?

JEWISH GENTLEMAN

If they can sleep through each other's snoring, they can
sleep through anything. Sing softly.

GREEK GENTLEMAN

Very well. (Sings.) "Golden Apollo——" (He breaks off; to
JOSEPH, politely.) You will excuse my singing about Apollo.
The words are of no importance, but the tune is pretty.
(Sings.)

> Golden Apollo,
>   lord of the burning bow,
> Thy brow with sacred fillets bound
> And deathless laurel crowned;
> Singer and seer, whose splendour lights the sun,
> Sweet, terrible one!
> Swift as the swallow
>   thy searching arrows go.
> Then smite, lord, smite the heart of desire
> With thy celestial fire.

{The CENTURION comes in, right, and speaks to the SENTRY,
who wakes his companion to go on guard in his place. The CEN-
TURION picks his way slowly across the stage, lending momentary
attention to the song and going to stand by entrance, left.}

> Master of vision
>   throned on the circling wheel,
> Immortal born of mortal birth

174

That once didst visit earth
And as a servant humbly walk with men;
Turn, turn thee again,
Mighty physician
　　　Whose hand can harm and heal,
And quench, lord, quench thy heavenly dart
For it doth rive the heart.
{MERCHANT *rolls over with a loud snore and snort; they all
laugh.*}

JEWISH GENTLEMAN

There is the comment of the commercial mind. You may
rive his ears, but never his heart. Try again.

GREEK GENTLEMAN

There is no more to that song. Take the lute yourself.

JEWISH GENTLEMAN

I will sing you an old Jewish tale. *(Sings. After verse 1, the
other two join in the chorus.)*

　　　　Adam and Eve stood under a tree,
　　　　　　(Four rivers in Paradise)
　　　　A sweet and comely sight to see
　　　　For they were fair as fair could be,
　　　　Adam and Eve beneath the tree
　　　　　　(Paradise, Paradise,
　　　　　　God is all in all).

　　　　And on the tree the branches grew
　　　　　　(Four rivers in Paradise)
　　　　Adorned with leaves of tender hue,
　　　　And they were fair as fair could be
　　　　and Adam and Eve stood under the tree
　　　　　　(Paradise, Paradise,
　　　　　　God is all in all).

{*An ox lows.*}

JOSEPH

Listen! What was that?

175

GREEK GENTLEMAN

Only an ox lowing. Sing the next verse.

JEWISH GENTLEMAN (sings)

And on the branch a beauteous flower
(Four rivers in Paradise)
Budded and bloomed from hour to hour,
The flower that on the branches grew
Adorned with leaves of tender hue,
And it was fair as fair could be
And Adam and Eve stood under the tree
(Paradise, Paradise,
God is all in all).
{CENTURION goes out, left.}
And in that flower a fruit of gold
(Four rivers in Paradise)
Lay hid within the petals' fold,
The petals of the beauteous flower
That budded and bloomed from hour to hour,
The flower that on the branches grew
Adorned with leaves of tender hue,
And it was fair as fair could be
And Adam and Eve stood under the tree
(Paradise, Paradise,
God is all in all).
{An ass brays.}

JOSEPH

Listen again.

GREEK GENTLEMAN

It is only the braying of an ass. Go on. Never mind the competition.

JEWISH GENTLEMAN (sings)

But Eve put forth her hand anon,
(Four rivers in Paradise)
And bit that fruit unto the stone,
The strange, forbidden fruit of gold

That hid within the petals' fold,
The petals of the beauteous flower
That budded and bloomed from hour to hour,
The flower that on the branches grew
Adorned with leaves of tender hue,
And the tree withered down to the ground so bare,
And Adam and Eve stood naked there;
>*(Paradise, Paradise,*
>*God is all in all).*

But when the stone had fallen to earth,
>*(Four rivers in Paradise)*
It brought another tree to birth,
That tall and stately grew anon,
The tree that sprang from that fruit stone,
The strange forbidden fruit of gold
That hid within the petals' fold,
The petals of the beauteous flower
That budded and bloomed from hour to hour,
The flower that on the branches grew
Adorned with leaves of tender hue,
And it was fair as fair could be,
And Adam and Eve stood under the tree
>*(Paradise, Paradise,*
>*God is all in all).*

GREEK GENTLEMAN

Well sung, all! There is nothing like music to pass the time
away. How goes the night?
>{CENTURION *reappears, left (L.U.).*}

JOSEPH

It is the dark hour before the dawn. Hark!
>{*The cry of the Child is heard.*}

JEWISH GENTLEMAN

That sounds more like it. Congratulations, carpenter.
>{*Enter* LANDLADY *from stable.*}

177

GREEK GENTLEMAN

Here comes our good hostess, grinning from ear to ear. How about it, mistress? What's the news?

LANDLADY

Come hither, Master Carpenter, and see! Your good lady is lighter of a splendid son.

JOSEPH

Praise be to God!

JEWISH GENTLEMAN

I should have lost my bet. Congratulations again. So you were lending a hand after all, hostess? You seem very much pleased about it all.
{CENTURION *works his way down on left.*}

LANDLADY

Well, sir, when it comes to babies, even innkeepers has their feelings. And the dear mother is such a sweet person—it's a pleasure to do anything for her. A beautiful child, and both doing fine. Come along, father, and have a look. You'll be that proud you won't know yourself.

JOSEPH

The dayspring from on high hath visited us.
{JOSEPH *follows the* LANDLADY *into the stable. The* CENTURION *crosses briskly left to right in front of the platform.*}

JEWISH GENTLEMAN

Well, well—that bit of excitement's over. Hullo, Centurion, you still on the prowl? Have you heard the glad tidings? The carpenter's wife has presented him with a son.

CENTURION

The gods be favourable to the boy!

GREEK GENTLEMAN

And there you are! Kingdoms rise and fall, wars are waged, politicians wrangle, trade suffers, poor men starve, philsophers exchange insults and agree in nothing except that times are very evil and mankind rapidly going to the dogs. And yet, when one more soul is born into this highly unsatisfactory world, everybody conspires to be delighted.

JEWISH GENTLEMAN

And every time his parents are persuaded that he's going to turn out something wonderful, whereas, if they only knew it, he's destined, as likely as not, to finish up between two thieves on Crucifixion Hill. It all makes me feel very old and disillusioned.

CENTURION

Don't you worry, sir. You'll get younger as you get older.

GREEK GENTLEMAN

At any rate, I suppose we can now hope for a little sleep.
   {Knocking at the gate.}
Oh, Hades!

VOICE (without)

Now then, what the devil do you want?

VOICES (without)

Let us in! Let us in! We have news, news, news!

CENTURION

News? What does that mean? (Shouting.) Porter! open the gates! (Softly.) Might be a rebellion. You never know. Look alive there! (He moves up behind the two GENTLEMEN. The 1ST SOLDIER springs to his feet and joins the 2ND SOLDIER at the entrance. The LANDLADY enters from the stable, and the LAND-LORD from the left.)

179

LANDLORD

A rebellion? God forbid! *(Shouting.) Keep the gate shut!*

LANDLADY

Oh, please, dear Captain, don't let them in! We shall all be murdered in our beds.

CENTURION

If there is news, we must hear it. *(Shouting.)* Open the gate.
{*Gate unbarred. SHEPHERDS enter noisily; the SOLDIERS bar their way.*}
Now, then, fellows! What's all this noise about? *(He signs to the SOLDIERS to let them through. They stand guard again behind the SHEPHERDS.)*

SHEPHERDS

Show us the Child that is born to-night! For we have seen a miracle.

MERCHANT *(waking suddenly)*

Hey! hey! Robbers! murder! help! Keep off! Let me go!
I'm only a poor traveller! I've no money on me! Help! help!
{*Everybody wakes up. Tumult.*}
{*Bring SHEPHERDS centre and bring up arena flood slowly to full during their story.*}

CENTURION

Be quiet, there!

JEWISH GENTLEMAN

It's all right, Aaron ben Isaac. Nobody's being robbed.

LANDLORD

You've had nightmare.

GREEK GENTLEMAN

It's only some shepherds, who say they've seen a miracle.

MERCHANT

Miracle, indeed! I thought I was being murdered. This inn is disgracefully run. I shall complain to the authorities.

1ST SHEPHERD

Indeed, indeed, sirs, a wonderful thing is come to pass.

MERCHANT

Oh, go to Gehenna! *(He rolls himself up again and resolutely closes his ears.)*

CENTURION

Quick, fellows! Your story.

1ST SHEPHERD

Sir, we were in the fields, keeping watch over our sheep this night. And as I sat, looking eastward toward Beth-Shemesh, I beheld a great light, as though the sun were rising an hour before its time. And even while I looked, my son Matthew spoke to me, and said: Father, said he, what is this? Is the sun rising in the west? Then I turned myself about, and saw as it might be a ring of fire, all about the earth, and the hills and trees glowing like copper in the furnace.

2ND SHEPHERD

Ay, and the fire burnt up and up to the very pole, putting out the stars.

3RD SHEPHERD

And out of the fire, out of the sky—I cannot tell how, but so it was—there came an angel, great and terrible and shining. And we were sore afraid.

2ND SHEPHERD

Ay, that we were. But the sheep weren't afraid, not they. And that's a strange thing too.

1ST SHEPHERD

Then the angel spoke, clear as anything. "Be not afraid," he says, "for behold I bring you glad tidings of great joy which shall be to you and all people. For to you," he says, "is born this day in the City of David"—that's here, sir, you know—"a saviour, which is the Lord Messiah."

JEWISH GENTLEMAN

You hear, Philip? The Lord Christ. Zadok the Pharisee should be listening to this. What's become of him, by the way?

GREEK GENTLEMAN

Oh, he cast himself into outer darkness some time ago.

JEWISH GENTLEMAN

"Joy to all people"—you are sure the angel said, "to *all* people"?

1ST SHEPHERD

Certain sure, sir. And we was just thinking as how there might be a many babes born in the city, and how was we to know, when he says, "This," he says, "shall be a sign to you. Ye shall find the babe wrapped in swaddling clothes and lying in a manger." So I looks at Sam, and Sam looks at me, and then, all of a sudden we sees the heavens open and thousands, ah! millions of angels, more than a man could count and singing that beautiful—Oh, sirs, listen! listen! There it be again—going right away over the roof, as clear as clear.

ANGELS' CHOIR *(distant)*

Glory to God in the highest and in earth peace, goodwill towards men.
{*Repeat chorus, crescendo and dying away again; dim arena flood to about quarter as song passes.*
Pause.}

CENTURION

Look here, I don't understand a word of all this.

1ST SHEPHERD

Couldn't you hear nothing?

CENTURION

Not a word.

GREEK GENTLEMAN

Nothing whatever.

LANDLADY

They've had too much to drink, that's what it is. You didn't ought to have given them that wine, sir.

JEWISH GENTLEMAN

I don't know. I fancy I did hear something—but it was very faint.

CENTURION

This is all a pack of nonsense. Go home, you shepherds, and let's hear no more of this. *(He turns to the* TRAVELLERS, *who are beginning to talk.)* Quiet, everybody. Get back to bed. Show's over.
    {*The* TRAVELLERS *subside.*}

1ST SHEPHERD

But may we not see the Child?

CENTURION *(after a brief hesitation)*

You may see him. But for his own sake, don't let your story come to King Herod's ears.

JEWISH GENTLEMAN

Come with me, shepherds. I'll show you the way. *(He leads the SHEPHERDS up centre.)* Listen! That is the Mother singing to her son.

{*The CENTURION sits on edge of platform, a menacing black shadow between the audience and the brazier.*
The curtain before the stable-door is withdrawn to disclose the HOLY FAMILY. (Take out spot batten.)
The GREEK GENTLEMAN (lost in the shadows) has picked up the lute and accompanies MARY's song.}

MARY *(sings)*

Balow-la-lee, my little king,
What shall we do to comfort Thee?
Canst Thou for whom the angels sing
Content Thee with balow-la-lee,
Balow-la-lee?
Balow-la-lee, my royal child,
There's little we can give to Thee,
A manager-bed, a mother mild,
The ox and the ass for company,
Balow-la-lee.

{1ST *and* 3RD SHEPHERDS *on the side of stable-door;* 2ND SHEPHERD *and* JEWISH GENTLEMAN *on the other.*}

1ST SHEPHERD

Your pardon, mistress. May we come in and see the Baby?

MARY

Surely, good shepherds. Come in and welcome.

JOSEPH

Tread softly. Do not wake Him.

MARY

He is already awake. Look, He is smiling at you.

1ST SHEPHERD

All hail, little king! See, here is a woollen fleece to be your royal robe.

2ND SHEPHERD

All hail, little king! Here is a shepherd's crook, to be your royal sceptre.

3RD SHEPHERD

All hail, little king! Here is a twist of flowering thorn to be your royal crown.

MARY

My Son shall remember you all when He comes into His kingdom.

JEWISH GENTLEMAN

Madam, I fear I have come unprovided. I was not expecting a revelation. But if ever your Son and I should meet again, I will have a rich gift ready for him.

MARY

Sir, we shall not forget your goodwill. What is your name?

JEWISH GENTLEMAN

I am Joseph of Arimathaea.
{*The* SHEPHERDS *play a pastoral tune upon their pipes, and the Tableaux Curtains close. From behind:* Landlord! landlord! . . . Up, you lazy slaves! will you lie there till noonday? . . . Saddle the asses and bring my reckoning. . . . Oh, dear, I never got a wink of sleep all night. . . . Has anybody seen my slippers? . . . Confound you, sir, you've knocked my flask over. . . . Git over, hoss—ah! would you then? . . . You have overcharged me by five pence. . . . Landlord! landlord! *(fading away.)*}
{*If gauzes are used, drop them on* NATIVITY TABLEAU, *black-out, and let voices fade off in the dark; then bring up spot on fore-stage as* KINGS *re-enter.*}

BALTHAZAR

Caspar!

CASPAR

Melchior!

MELCHIOR

Balthazar!

CASPAR

I looked for wisdom—and behold! the wisdom of the innocent.

MELCHIOR

I looked for power—and behold! the power of the helpless.

BALTHAZAR

I looked for the manhood in God—and behold! a God made man.

CASPAR

Up and to horse! Make haste! for the Star has moved on before us
And the east is pale with the dawn. We must ride by faith.

MELCHIOR

Following the light invisible.

BALTHAZAR

Following the Star.

Curtain
(or, if there is no front curtain, the Kings go out left)

FINIS

PLANS FOR AMATEUR PRODUCTION

BY

MICHAEL WOLFE

Some General Remarks on
Drops and Curtains

Both of these plays are designed with a playing area surrounded by three walls made out of painted drops (suspended cloth). These walls serve two purposes: they suggest locale and mood for the plays, and they screen off the backstage areas. The simplest way to provide a simulated wall in a set is to hang a painted piece of material from a taut line; in essence, a sheet hung from a clothes line.

As with a clothes line, the biggest problem is finding a structure stong enough to withstand the force exerted by the weight on the line. For this, four corner posts are needed. (Their construction will be discussed later.) The corner posts closest to the audience (downstage) will also serve to help support side curtains which block off the backstage area from the audience. Old draperies or curtains of dark and heavy material serve best for these curtains. They should extend from the corners of the stage to the walls of the existing room (or very close to the walls) where they should be fastened in a way we will leave to your ingenuity. (It depends a great deal on what kind of walls there are in the room you are using for a theatre.)

Preparing the Drops for Painting

As we said earlier, the walls of both plays are simulated by painted cloth. For either play you will need four light canvas painters' drop cloths. These most commonly come in a 9' x 12' size that will do nicely. You will also need three 20' lengths of study 3/8" non-stretching rope. While you are shopping, you might as well pick up several spools of button thread and a couple of heavy-duty needles, since the sewing is best done by hand. You will also need a large roll of wide masking tape.

THE DEVIL TO PAY: Cut one of the cloths into three equal pieces (9' x 4'). Sew each of the strips to the three larger pieces so that you will have three drops, each measuring 9' x 16'.

HE THAT SHOULD COME: This play calls for two standard 9' x 12' cloths for the side drops. But, since the back drop should be a 9' x 16' "wall", an extra strip of 9' x 4' cut from the fourth canvas cloth will have to be sewn on. (Overlap the edges of the strips 1/4" before sewing, but do not turn the canvas under.)

FOR BOTH PLAYS: The pieces of canvas may be sewn together with large stitches such as you might use for basting. (Be sure to use heavy-duty button thread.) After sewing the pieces together, stitch a 4" hem along the top edge of the canvas over the rope. Please note that, although your walls will eventually be 8' high, at this stage of the game you will have extra material at the bottom. *Do not cut this off!*

Cutting the Openings in the Canvas

THE DEVIL TO PAY: As you will note on the groundplan, *The Devil to Pay* has five entrances to the stage: the fireplace and door (stageright), the door and magic mirror (back drop), and the large stained glass window (stageleft). All of these openings, except the magic mirror, can be formed by having vertical slits cut in the canvas. The two doorways may also be formed by cutting away all the canvas in the openings. The magic mirror should be left uncut until the actual setting up of the drops.

To cut slits, start with the fireplace by taking one of the canvasses and laying it on the floor. This will be your stageright wall. Next decide which side of the canvas will be nearest to the audience (downstage). From that side measure in 6'3" at several widely spaced points and mark these with a pencil. Draw a vertical line connecting the points going from the top of your drop to the bottom. Make an X on this line 4' from the top of the canvas. Then take your scissors and boldly, but carefully, cut a slit along the line from the bottom of the canvas to the X.

For the slit in the door on the same wall, measure in 2'8" from the opposite side (the side of the canvas that will be furthest from the audience). Again mark at several points and draw a top to bottom vertical line connecting the points. Measure 1' down from the top and make an X. Again, cut a slit along the line to the X near the top. Stitch across the top of all slits several times to retard fraying and bind edges with masking tape.

Lay a second piece of canvas down to work on the slit for the door in the back drop. Decide which side will be nearer to the wall with the stained glass windows, and then use the same measuring, marking, and line-drawing technique. Measure in 3'9" from the stageleft side and 6" from the top. Cut, stitch and bind as before.

The last canvas to be cut is the one with the stained glass windows (stageleft). The measuring on the stageleft canvas is done from the side nearest the audience (downstage). Measure in 5'9" and 4" down from the top. Then follow the same cutting, sewing and binding procedure as above.

If you want to make full openings for the doorways, carefully cut away the canvas in each doorway after having drawn the openings on the drop. The new edges should be bound with masking tape, and later painted to match the trim. These realistic-sized door openings will allow for easier entrances and exits, but they add another problem: now you must mask off the backstage area from the sight of the audience. Do this with some sort of suspended drape or curtain.

HE THAT SHOULD COME: As you will note on the groundplan, *He That Should Come* has four archway-entrances to the stage. The actual entrances can be formed two ways: by cutting vertical slits in the canvas in the center of each archway, or by cutting away all the canvas in the openings.

If you want to cut slits, start with the wall without the fountain (stageright). Take one of your 9' x 12' canvasses and lay it on the floor. Next, decide which side of the canvas will be nearest to the audience (downstage). From that side, measure in 2' at several widely spaced points and mark with a pencil. Draw a vertical line connecting the points, going from the top of your drop to the bottom. Make an X on this line 1' from the top of the canvas. Then take your scissors and boldly, but carefully, cut a slit along the line from the bottom of the canvas to the X.

Since the second arch on that wall is exactly the same size, go to the opposite end of the same canvas (the side of the canvas that will be furthest from the audience) and do exactly the same thing, using the same measurement. Stitch across the top edge of the slits several times to retard fraying. Finally, take the masking tape and bind the slit edges. Set that piece aside.

Lay the canvas that measures 9' x 16' down to work on the back drop. Measure in 8' from either end, since the arch is located in the middle of the drop. Again mark at several points and draw a vertical line from the top of the drop to the bottom, connecting the points. Measure 6″ down from the top and make an X. Again, cut a slit along the line to the X at the top. Stitch and bind as before and set that piece aside.

The last canvas to be cut is the other 9′ x 12′ drop. This is the one with the fountain (stageleft). Using the same measuring, marking, and line-drawing technique, decide which side will be furthest from the audience and measure in 2′ from that side. Measure down 1′ from the top, then follow the same procedure as above for the slit.

If you want to make full openings for these archways, carefully cut away the canvas in each doorway after having drawn the openings on the drop. The edges of each opening should then be bound with masking tape, and later painted to match the arch trim. These realistic-sized openings will allow for easier entrances and exits, but they add another problem: now you must mask off the backstage area from the sight of the audience. Do this with some sort of suspended drape or curtain.

Shopping for Paint

All the paints used should be water base paints. They will wash off hands and brushes and sometimes clothing when still wet, but when dry, they are permanent.

FOR BOTH PLAYS:
1 gallon of a cheap, flat, white acrylic paint (latex, vinyl, acrylic, etc.) for the prime coat and for spattering.
1 gallon of a stone gray (medium gray with a touch of brown). To avoid having to mix paints, try to find this color in a paint store. It is a few shades lighter than battleship gray, about half-way between off-white and charcoal gray, only warmer.
1 gallon flat black acrylic.
3 pounds flameproofing powder (see flameproofing section and the list of theatrical suppliers).
1 4″ brush for spattering (wash well with warm water and dishwashing detergent after every use).
2 cheap rollers (1 for prime and 1 for base). Tell store it must be "suitable for latex paint". (If you don't think you can roll a complete coat on all drops in one day, then buy the throwaway kind.)

1 gallon white glue (Elmer's Glue). Don't be concerned about the use of this. It will all be explained in due time.

THE DEVIL TO PAY:

From 2 quarts to 1 gallon charcoal acrylic.
1 pint each of red, blue, yellow, brown, and green poster paint.
1 tube of silver acrylic artist's paint.

HE THAT SHOULD COME:

1 gallon of charcoal acrylic.

Applying the Prime and Base Coats

The first step in the painting procedure is to apply the prime coat to all the drops which you have prepared. Take the can of flat white acrylic paint and thin it slightly by adding no more than one cup of water to the gallon. It can then be rolled on thinly and evenly. Pay special attention to seams, hems, and stitching, etc., and keep the paint off the rope ends.

After the prime coat is dry, open the gallon of stone gray paint. This will be used for the base coat.

THE DEVIL TO PAY: While someone is putting the base coat on the other two walls, set aside the wall that is to be used for the stained glass windows. It is necessary to make a pencil outline of the stained glass window areas since they should not have a base coat. (See section on grid.) Once the windows have been outlined, you may paint the base coat on the rest of that drop.

HE THAT SHOULD COME: Apply the base coat to all of each drop.

Using a Grid to Copy and Enlarge

BOTH PLAYS: A grid consists of nothing more than penciled squares which you mark off first on a tracing of the wall elevations in the book and then—to scale—on the drops themselves. It is the method by which you transfer both large outlines (doors, windows, etc.) and smaller details to the drops. The basic grid is made up of squares measuring 1' x 1' on the canvas. Where there are no details, this grid is all you will need. Where there is a great deal of detail, you may subdivide the squares into smaller squares as many times as you need.

Start by taking a piece of tracing paper and carefully tracing the outlines of the wall elevations as given in the book. Then, using a ruler and a triangle or T-square, divide the tracing of the wall elevation into 3/8" squares. Each of these squares will equal one square foot on your canvas wall.

Lay a canvas drop that has been basecoated with paint on the floor. (Don't worry too much yet about walking on it.) Each canvas has a little extra at the bottom which you will later use to make it taut, but this means that you should start measuring from the *top* of each wall when you mark the canvas into 1' squares. Pencil is best for marking.

After you have marked both your tracing and the wall into squares, you are ready to transfer the major outlines. The general idea is to locate where the lines cross into and out of each square on your tracing, and then connect them so that you have an enlarged version of the drawing in the book, ready for painting.

THE DEVIL TO PAY: These drops have a great deal of detail. Drawings of each of the windows, doors, book cases, etc., will be found scattered throughout the pages of the script. These detailed drawings are exactly twice the size of the outlines shown on the wall elevations. Therefore, make a tracing paper grid of 3/4" squares (instead of 3/8") so that each of these squares will equal 1' on the canvas. Then, with another color pencil, divide each square into four 3/8" squares. (These will be 6" squares on the drop.) Carefully trace the details onto the paper grid.

Unfortunately, when you attempt to transfer these details to the drops, you will find that the edges of windows and doors, etc., are not apt to fall exactly on one of your basic 1' grid lines *on the canvas*. Therefore, you will have to *ignore* the basic grid on the canvas and make independent ones within your outlines. Colored pencils may help to avoid confusion, and it really won't be that confusing once you get started.

Do not worry too much about fine details on the canvas at this stage. A good eye and a hand with a paintbrush can bring out a great deal later. Remember that only what is big will "read" onstage.

Using a template for the scallops around the magic mirror will save much toil and trouble. Cut one piece of wood or cardboard to the right size and shape and use it to trace each scallop.

HE THAT SHOULD COME: If you find that you need more guidance than can be provided by your 1' squares, you may subdivide them, but this will probably not be necessary. Do not worry if the stones are not very regular in shape. If the arches and the fountain give you some trouble, try plotting several of the points on the curve and then experiment with a compass made of string and a pencil.

Painting

Previously, we got as far as applying the prime and base coats to the drops. Assuming that these are dry and the drawing has been transferred, you may paint the details.

Now is the time to use the mysterious gallon of white glue you bought. This should be mixed with the poster paints to prevent the paint from flaking off whenever anyone bumps into the canvas. Get a number of large and medium-sized jars in which to keep the various color mixtures. Mix one part glue to two parts poster paint. Mix them well. Some of the colors may lighten with the addition of glue; if so, increase the amount of paint. The mixed glue and paint should be stirred often while in use and be covered tightly at night. Should a skin form by morning, remove it carefully. If the mixture thickens too much, add a few tablespoons of water, and mix again.

Once the colors are applied, it is time to spatter the set—that is, to add shape and shadows to break up the visual flatness by applying tiny spatters of paint. These will be white or black. Follow the instructions given for each play. The canvas drops should be hung vertically for this operation, and the ropes through the tops should be drawn as taut as possible. To spatter, take a dry brush (a brush lightly dipped in paint and scraped so that it will not drip) and hit the handle, sending droplets of paint onto the canvas. This sounds difficult, but is easy once you get the hang of it. Practice on newspapers until you can control the spread and size of the dots (they should be no bigger that 1/8″ in diameter). It's better to take your time and have very tiny dots than to have ugly drips running down the canvas drops.

Finally, use the flat black paint to paint the back sides of the slit flaps so no bare canvas will show.

THE DEVIL TO PAY: First, paint all the "wood" trim with a rich, dark brown (add yellow to brown until you have a satisfactory color), including the strip around the stained glass windows, the cabinet doors, the bookcases and the door trim. Then the snakes, dragons and scallops on the trim should be done in mustard yellow. Use charcoal gray for the mortar lines in the stonework of the fireplace, for the openings of the doorways and fireplaces, and for the leading of the stained glass windows. The sconces should be basecoated charcoal gray with white candles and yellow flames. To get the pounded pewter look, dab the corner of a sponge in white paint and splotch it on. Outline the sconce scallops in black. The books can be multicolored but muted— dark greens, dark reds, grays, blues and black. Use dark green for the chart holder, white for the charts, skulls and bottles, black for the eclipse chart with white lettering, and realistic colors for the earth, moon and sun. For the stained glass windows use bright primary colors, plus sky blue and pink. Remember—you want to tone down all parts of the set except the stained glass windows, leaving them to stand out, especially when lit. Don't be afraid of making the set too spooky. Use your imagination and have fun with it.

Spatter and shadow the stonework of the fireplace with flat black paint. Spatter the openings of the doors with white paint, and that of the fireplace with black. Once the canvas drops are set up together as if for performance, downplay the corners of the set by spattering. The walls should get darker in the corners and lighter away from them.

HE THAT SHOULD COME: Use charcoal gray for the mortar lines around the stonework, keeping the thickness of the line reasonably constant. Thicken the lines for the stones that frame the doorways, as well as those around the arch over the window on the back drop and the fountain on the stageleft drop. The door and window openings should be painted charcoal gray also. Using flat black paint, lightly spatter all stonework. Then use this technique to bring out the shadows indicated on the fountain. Once the canvas drops are set up as if for performance, downplay the corners of the set by spattering. The walls should get darker in the corners and lighter away from them. Using a clean brush and flat white paint, spatter the doorways and windows very sparingly. This will add illusionary depth to the openings.

A Note on Flameproofing

In a later section, several theatrical supply companies are listed. Many of them can supply you with the proper flameproofing chemical to use on your drops. Generally the chemical is sold as a powder, one pound of which will make a gallon when mixed with water. This amount will cover 12 to 20 square yards, therefore you will need 3 pounds for either play. You can make one gallon of flameproofing compound by mixing one pound of sal ammoniac, one pound of borax and three quarts of water. Both of these compounds are highly corrosive to such varied substances as metals and human skin, so be very careful.

To apply, mix the flamproofing solution and spray it onto both sides of the drops with pump sprayer, which is similar to a garden insecticide sprayer.

Remember—flameproofing is one of your most important set preparations. Throughout history, some of the most disastrous fires have been in theaters. So be safe, and be sure to flameproof your drops after painting them.

Corner Posts

The corner post as drawn will work for both stageright corners of the stage. The two posts for stageleft should be constructed as mirror images (see sketch). The grooves in the top are to align the rope used to support the side and back drops. The ropes should pass through their grooves and be tied off to a cleat somewhere on the vertical 2 x 4. The legs of these posts should be made as secure as possible. Sandbags or concrete blocks will serve well, but be sure to make all the actors and backstage personnel aware of these potential toe-stubbers. If a particular triangular plywood corner brace is in the way of an exit, it may be cut back along the line of the bottom 2 x 4 as necessary. If any of the wood shows, it should be painted the colors of the drops.

Finishing and Securing the Drops

While doing the final painting of the drops, you probably noticed that there was extra canvas along all of the bottom edges. You will need some of this, so don't cut it all off. Measure down from the top line 8' at all corners and mark these points on the back. Repeat this marking 3' from each corner. Where you made slits, make similar marks for each slit opening, one on either side of the slit where the visual "opening" starts. Now carefully cut away the excess cloth along the bottom of these "openings" so that they just meet the floor. (If you cut away all the canvas in an opening, the previous operation is not necessary.) Then cut away half the excess 3' in from each corner (strips about 4" x 3').

The remaining full sections of extra canvas now hanging will be used to help secure the drops. Cut pieces of 2 x 4 corresponding to the length of each section along the floor. Fold each section under and back so that it cannot be seen from the playing area, and place each cut 2 x 4 on its corresponding section. There should be about 4-1/2" of canvas sticking out from under the edge of the wood. Wrap this snugly back over the 2 x 4 and tack or staple it onto the wood. The weight of these pieces of wood resting on the floor will help stabilize the walls of the set. If the 2 x 4's near a slit opening tend to slide, use sandbags or bricks to hold them in place. If the bottom corners within 3' of the corner posts flap too much, add short sections of 2 x 2's in the same way you did with the 2 x 4's above, or staple them to the corner braces where possible.

THE DEVIL TO PAY: Carefully cut out the magic mirror section of the back drop. Tape the edges of the canvas and paint them to match the drop. Now construct the magic mirror following the directions in the next section.

THE DEVIL TO PAY: To build the magic mirror, make a frame out of 1 x 4's with 1 x 3's for triangular floor bracing, as illustrated. The dimensions of the frame should be 3'1 1/2" x 6'6".

Stretch lightweight unbleached muslin lightly over the frame and staple it onto the frame on all edges. Squeeze a small amount of silver acrylic artist's paint from a tube, add a touch of white glue and thin with water so that you may apply a transparent coating. The paint should be so thin that you can still see through the weave of the muslin. Spatter the silvered muslin with black paint (see painting section). When dry, make a number of diagonal streaks in black paint, using a small brush and quick strokes. (See drawing of mirror on p. 212). Then pencil vertical lines on the back of the muslin. These should be 3" apart. Start 6" from the top and continue to the floor. Then cut slits along each line with a mat knife. Remove the staples from the bottom edge and reinforce the top and side staples. Now put the magic mirror in its opening in the back drop, and staple the edges of the drop to the frame to keep them from flapping. If the frame itself is unstable, use sandbags on the 1 x 3 legs (see sketch).

You should now be able to pass through the mirror as you would through a bead curtain. If the paint hasn't added enough weight to keep the mirror from moving with each breeze, attach a small weight to each strand. Someone standing behind the mirror should be visible only when directly lit from behind the muslin.

HE THAT SHOULD COME: Construction of the well and the wall fragment is basically the same (see sketches). The tops, 3/4" plywood, are cut first and the 2 x 4's are cut to frame the tops. The framing pieces are nailed together and then the tops are glued to the frame with white glue and nailed on. The framed tops are then flipped over and the 2 x 4 legs are nailed on. The side facing can be any cheap, thin, rigid material. Heavy cardboard is excellent. So that the facing will not flap at the bottom, first nail several small pieces of scrap wood near the bottom and on the outside of each leg. The thickness of the scraps should be (or total) about 1 1/2". The side facing may then be glued and nailed on. When fully assembled, the edges of these set pieces should be lightly rounded with a file or rasp, then basecoated and painted to look like stone, the way you painted the back and side drops.

Props

THE DEVIL TO PAY: Whenever possible, the props and set decorations for this play should be weird, old-fashioned and slightly exaggerated. On the stage, only the blatant and unsubtle will seem real enough. A few specifics to help set the mood: the books, especially the large book of magic, should be the size of large hardbound atlases, but dusty and well worn. The parchments and the devil's bond should be sheets of heavy drawing paper, 11" x 14" or larger, which have been stained by dipping in tea. The tables should be cluttered with all sorts of bottles and flasks and books and papers. Most encyclopedias have pictures of alchemists and their laboratories which are useful guides to the decoration of this set. The tables for this set should be of heavy wood, as should the benches and the chair. All should look old, not polished.

HE THAT SHOULD COME: Most of the props needed for this play are related to people traveling. You'll need bedrolls, pots and pans, baskets, canvas and leather goods tied with rope or leather strapping—items which haven't changed much in 2000 years. Be more concerned that the objects look used and travel-worn than that they be authentic ancient Palestinian.

Special Effects

THE DEVIL TO PAY: In this very magical play, most effects can be achieved without too great an effort. The one exception is fire. The hell fire can be indicated reasonably well with lighting but candles, sconces, tapers and torches are another story. They are the bane of designers everywhere. Candles might be used in scene I, but be *very* cautious. Have buckets of water and sand readily available. And *never* use kerosene or any other form of wicked lamp near the stage or audience.

To make the "water steam up and bubble over", Wagner should bring a second flask down to Mephistopheles containing a chunk of dry ice, and empty it into the water contained in the flask held by Mephistopheles. For baggage to "waft in", it need merely be delivered by a devil in dark clothing.

As for sound effects, thunder may be achieved by shaking a 3' x 6' piece of sheet metal. Punch holes in the top of the sheet and suspend it with heavy twine or rope. Shake it brusquely from the bottom and leave it to calm itself. For "fire and explosion", use the metal sheet together with the lights (see the lighting section). Noises offstage of wheels, whips, snorts and flapping wings are best made by actors backstage with various props, noisemakers and their own voices. The key to "magic" of this sort is simplicity. Audiences will be more likely to accept and believe simple effects than the sound track from a Vincent Price movie.

HE THAT SHOULD COME: It is difficult for people to imitate animals, so the easiest way to have an ox low and an ass bray is to buy or borrow a sound effects record with barnyard animals on it. These records are generally available at record stores. If your record store cannot get one for you, contact one of the theatrical supply houses in the last section. Or contact your local radio station or your local library. They may let you borrow just the right record.

Stage Lighting

Stage lighting serves three basic functions: to light the actors, to help create or change a mood, and to create special effects where needed.

To fulfill these functions, you must call upon the materials and instruments you have on hand. Some auditoriums have no lighting beyond everyday fluorescent fixtures, while others have standard strip and footlights, usually with separate controls for red, white and blue colors. If you have no spotlights, you may want to build some "do-it-yourself" spotlights that are described later. Or perhaps you're lucky and have an auditorium with a full range of spot and flood lights and the capacity to plug them in and control them almost anywhere.

Our lighting plans call for the main frontal lights to be affixed to the same two downstage corner posts that support the side drops. If your stage is equipped with two freestanding light trees or light poles, you can use these instead of the corner posts. They should be placed just downstage of the corner posts. The special lights (Hell, Heaven and the mirror in "The Devil to Pay", and the tableau light for "He That Should Come") should be affixed to unmoving objects backstage of their openings. Tell the actors passing through the openings in the canvas and moving backstage to be sure that their motion does not shake the lights.

When running extension cords from the lights to the control area, be sure all wires are secured out of the way of actors and audience. Actors should be made aware of the fact that these cords will be carrying electricity during both rehearsal and show times. Since the backstage area will probably be quite dark, place low wattage (2 to 10 watt) lights near any obstructions. Night lights can serve this purpose. Place the light control area somewhere out of sight of the audience. And be sure to shield the light used by the light control person to read the script and cue sheets.

Various companies will lend, rent or sell you dimmer packs for selectively dimming the lights. If you want to build your own dimmers, have someone with electrical experience wire up several household dimmers (600 watts SCRs with punch-off control) with two standard two-prong Edison outlets each. Be sure that the box which contains these dimmers is always grounded.

The light plots for both plays give the color of the gel for each light by name and number. These names and numbers refer to plastic color media (gels) manufactured by Rosco Laboratories, Inc.. Known and sold as Roscolene, they are available in 20" x 24" sheets and are both heat resistant and waterproof. To purchase these gels, contact on of the companies listed in the last section.

To make "do-it-yourself" spotlights, you will need to buy 150 watt PAR 38 Spotlight Reflector Lamps. You can find them and the fixtures they need in a hardware store. The PAR bulb contains a parabolic reflector built right in and supplies a semi-focused, directional beam of light. Inexpensive swivel sockets with built-in clamps for mounting should be purchased, and some form of gel holder acquired. You can buy clip-on gel holders from a theatrical supply company (see later section) or you can make your own by attaching a 6" stovepipe or a two-pound coffee can (with both ends removed) to the clamp or socket with wire. If you are lucky, your hardware store will be able to sell you spring clip sockets for PARs with attached metal reflectors—the metal reflector will serve for a gel holder. The gel (color medium) must then be attached to the metal holder with a strong tape. Never tape the gel directly to the bulb as the heat of the bulb will melt or burn the gel and the tape. Also be careful when attaching the gel holder and make sure that none of the wire touches the "live" parts of the lamp.

The light plot for each play is designed to cover the major acting areas of the stage with directional and colored light so that the audience may both see and feel the actions and moods of the two plays. On the light plots, the arrows represent the direction of each light and the circles represent the area lit. (If you need to, prove this to yourself with a pencil and ruler drawing a longer line out from each arrow.) Some lights may be intended to cover more than one area, and some light will spill into other areas on stage. This is necessary to insure that all the stage is lit.

The light operator, together with the director, should work out specific cues and light levels for each scene or action. Do this by experimenting with the relative intensities of certain lights in each scene to help create a mood or to redirect the attention of the audience. Of course, the special effect lights should be used sparingly but as needed.

THE DEVIL TO PAY: Lights can be used very effectively in this play with so much magic and so many place and mood changes. Keep in mind that the fewer lights used in a scene, the more the imagination will fill in. By using the cooler lights (from stageleft) for most of a scene and then suddenly adding the warmer lights (from stageright) you can effectively move the scene from someplace mysterious to someplace warm and safe. Or by using all frontal lights equally and then fading out just the stageleft side (#5, #6, #7, #8) you can make the stage grow hotter and very strange (watch the shadows grow). Faustus can be almost totally isolated at center stage by using only lights #4 and #8. Of course, you will use the three special lights (Heaven, Hell and mirror) at appropriate times.

HE THAT SHOULD COME: To isolate the kings at the beginning, use light #6 alone, with the rest of the stage dark. When the main action of the play begins, use all the lights except the #7 special. As the play progresses, dim down #1 and #4 and slightly decrease the others. For the tableau of the Holy Family, fade up #1 and #4, illuminate #7 and fade out all others. Have the kings finish lit only with #3.

Understanding Stage Directions

Terms such as "stageleft" and "stageright" are used in the theatre to avoid misunderstandings or confusion, although these terms can be confusing until you are familiar with them. There are basically two points of view in a theatre, that of an actor and that of the audience: what appears on the audience's left is on the actor's right. Stage directions are from the actor's point of view. "Stageleft" is the left of an actor facing the audience while "stageright" is to his or her right. "Downstage" is the direction towards the audience. "Upstate" is towards the back of the theatre, away from the audience.

THE DEVIL TO PAY: The following chart should clarify Sayers' directions as they will be used on our set:

SAYERS' DIRECTION	WHAT THIS MEANS ON OUR SET
Mansion 1	Stageright (right drop)
Mansion 2	Stageright (right drop)
Mansion 3	Upleft (back drop)
Hell's Mouth	Fireplace
Above Hell's Mouth	Stageright (right drop)
Heaven	Stained glass windows
Exit right	Exit stageright (through right drop)
Exit left	Exit upleft (through back drop)

For instance the only people to move through the Fireplace are: Mephistopheles, Faustus and Devils. While the only people to move through the stained glass windows are Azrael, the Judge and Angels. The Magic Mirror is used as an entrance only once each by Faustus, Mephistopheles, Helen and Young Faustus. All other usages should be clear.

HE THAT SHOULD COME: Our set for this play resembles Sayers' description with one or two exceptions. The downstage left archway and the two secondary archways on the back drop have been eliminated. Downright still represents the gate and upleft still represents the way upstairs. The entire stage replaces her use of the rectangular platform. Her placement of characters fits well into this set if the Pharisee and the Landlord sit downleft on the stone wall instead of "a little right of centre".

Thus, at the beginning the Greek Gentleman enters downright; Roman soldiers are on boxes near downright; Pharisee and Landlord are on the stone wall downleft; Peasant Father, Mother and Boy are upright on the well; Husband and Wife are center left, behind the stone wall; the Merchant is upleft by the archway; and the Roman Centurion and Jewish Gentleman are up center in front of the back drop.

Adapting These Designs for High-Ceilinged Rooms

The back and side drops for these plays were kept at a height of 8' so that the plays could be performed in virtually any room. If you perform either play in a room with a very high ceiling, consider the following changes.

One possibility is to hang a banner 4' tall by 16' wide in midair directly over the back drop. This banner should have the name of the play boldly and neatly painted on in appropriate script.

Or cut and sew two 9' by 12' pieces of canvas so that your back drop will measure 16' across and be just under 12' tall. Two additional corner posts will be needed to support this new height. Be sure to spatter this new drop, especially the upper edge, so that the eye is not drawn up and away.

THE DEVIL TO PAY: If you add a banner, use German Gothic lettering for the name of the play. If you add height to the back drop, add another three rows of books.

HE THAT SHOULD COME: If you add a banner, use Bold Roman lettering for the name of the play. If you add height to the back drop, continue the stonework upward and add three evenly spaced arched windows along the new top edge.

For color gels, flameproofing, sound effects and much more:

Olesen Co. (mail order nationwide)
1535 Ivar Ave.
Hollywood, California 90028

Hub Electrical Co.
940 Industrial Drive
Elmhurst, Illinois 60126

Four star Stage Lighting
585 Gerard P.O. Box 800
Bronx, New York 10451

Four Star Stage Lighting
3935 North Mission
Los Angeles, California 90031

Little Stage Lighting Co.
10507 Hines Boulevard
Dallas, Texas 75220

Mole-Richardson Co.
937 North Sycamore Ave.
Hollywood, California 90038

Rosco Laboratories (color media, gels only)
11420 Ventura Boulevard
Studio City, California 91604

Stage Engineering and Supply, Inc.
P.O. Box 2002, 325 Karen Lane
Colorado Springs, Colorado 80901

Thomas Valentino (sound effects records)
15 West 46th Street
New York, New York 10036

Or look in the Yellow Pages of your phone book under: Theatrical Equipment and Supplies.

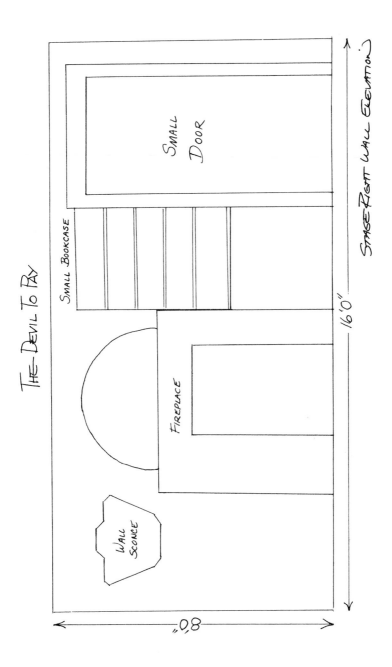

The Devil To Pay

Small Bookcase

Small Door

Fireplace

Wall Sconce

8'0"

16'0"

Stage Right Wall Elevation

207

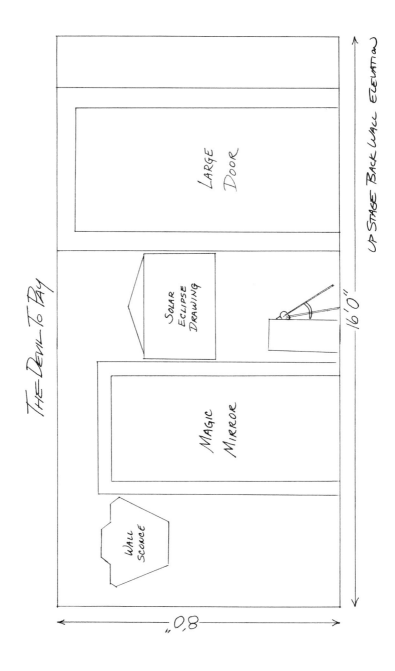

THE DEVIL TO PAY

LARGE DOOR

SOLAR ECLIPSE DRAWING

MAGIC MIRROR

WALL SCONCE

16' 0"

8' 0"

UP STAGE BACK WALL ELEVATION

208

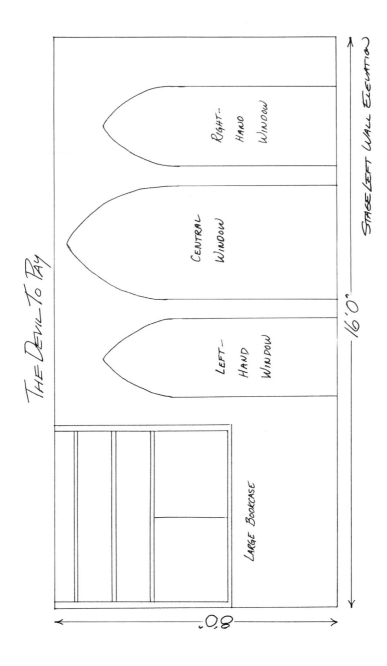

THE DEVIL TO PAY

RIGHT-HAND WINDOW

CENTRAL WINDOW

LEFT-HAND WINDOW

LARGE BOOKCASE

STAGE LEFT WALL ELEVATION

16'0"

8'0"

The Devil To Pay

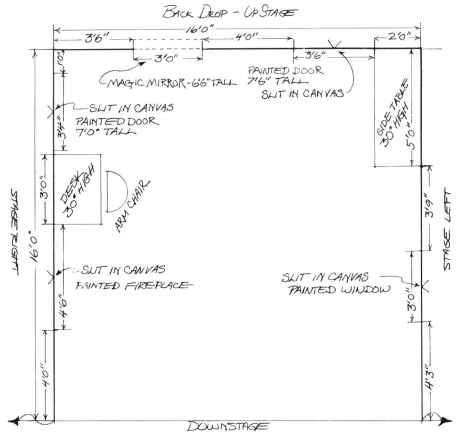

Back Drop - Up Stage

16'0" · 3'6" · 4'0" · 2'0"

3'0"

MAGIC MIRROR - 6'6" TALL

PAINTED DOOR 7'6" TALL
SLIT IN CANVAS · 3'6"

SLIT IN CANVAS
PAINTED DOOR 7'0" TALL · 3'4"

SIDE TABLE 30" HIGH · 5'0"

1'0"

DESK 30" HIGH · 3'0"

ARM CHAIR

STAGE RIGHT · 16'0"

STAGE LEFT · 3'9"

SLIT IN CANVAS
PAINTED FIREPLACE · 4'6"

SLIT IN CANVAS
PAINTED WINDOW · 3'0"

4'3"

4'0"

DOWNSTAGE

AUDIENCE

Groundplan —

NOTE: "SLITS" ARE ALWAYS IN EXACT CENTER OF PAINTED DOORWAYS, FIREPLACES, ETC. FOR MORE INFORMATION REFER TO SECTION OF TEXT ON PAINTING.

NOTE: SIDE CURTAINS ( ) EXTEND FROM "STAGE" TO WALLS OF ROOM.

NOTE: DESK SHOULD MEASURE 24" × 36" SIDE TABLE SHOULD MEASURE 24" × 60"

THESE DIMENSIONS ARE APPROXIMATE — IF YOUR FURNISHINGS ARE SMALLER ADJUST THE PAINTING TO FIT.

THE DEVIL TO PAY

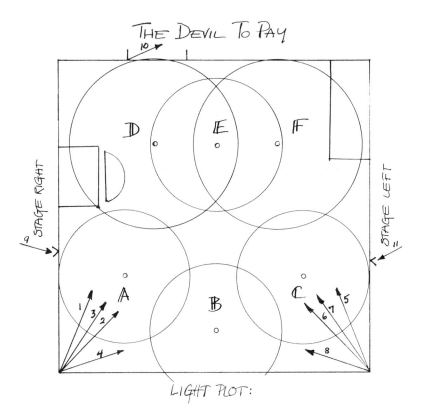

LIGHT PLOT:

LIGHT	LOCATED	AIMED AT	COLOR
1	STAGE RT.	D	B. AMBER .802
2	"	E F	S. PINK, 841
3	"	A	B. AMBER, 802
4	"	B C	S. PINK, 841
5	STAGE LFT.	F	ST. BLUE, 854
6	"	D E	ST. BLUE, 854
7	"	C	S. PINK, 841
8	"	B A	ST. BLUE, 854
9	BK. STAGE RT.	FIREPLACE	LT. RED, 821
10	BK. STAGE CEN.	MIRROR	FLESH PINK, 826
11	BK. STAGE LFT.	C. WINDOW	NO GEL

211

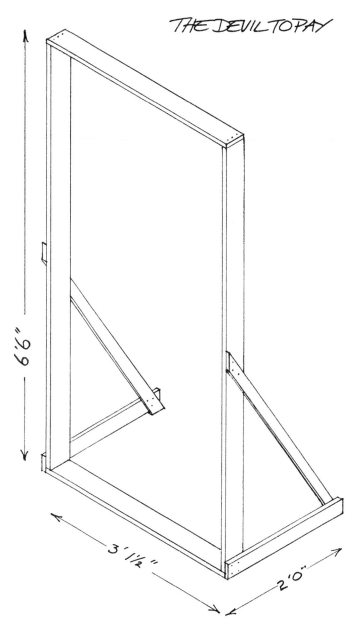

6'6"

3' 1½"

2'0"

CONSTRUCTION OF MAGIC MIRROR

NOTE

Detailed sketches of the scenic art for
THE DEVIL TO PAY may be found on
the following pages:

Page

1	Righthand window
2	Fireplace
6	Large bookcase
8	Lefthand window
10	Large door
18	Small bookcase
48	Umbrella stand
103	Drawing of solar eclipse
121	Wall sconce
122	Central window
188	Small door
212	Magic mirror

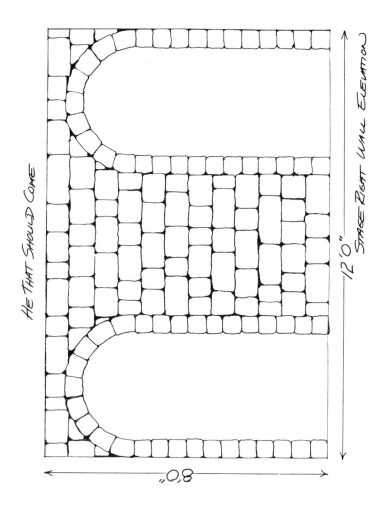

He That Should Come

12'0"   Stage Right Wall Elevation

8'0"

215

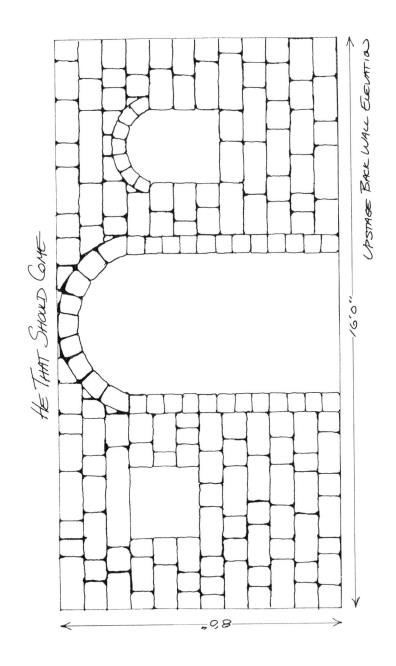

He That Should Come

Upstage Back Wall Elevation

16'0"

8'0"

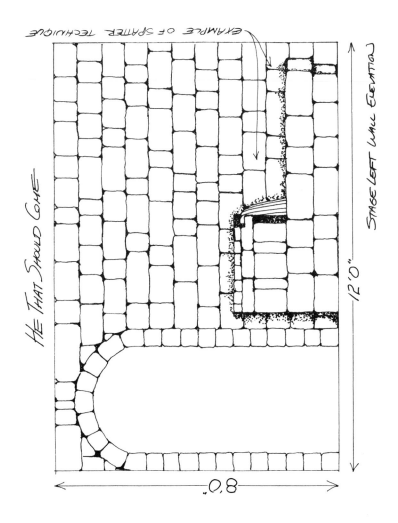

EXAMPLE OF SPATTER TECHNIQUE

STAGE LEFT WALL ELEVATION

HE THAT SHOULD COME

12'0"

8'0"

He That Should Come

Backdrop – Upstage

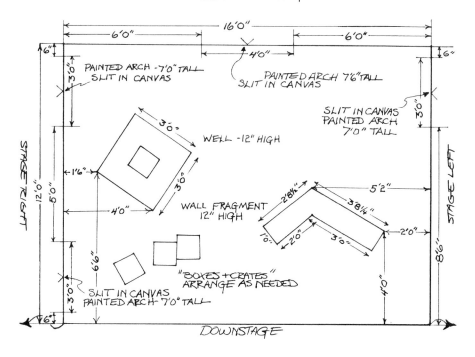

Groundplan —

NOTE: SIDE CURTAINS (⊿⊿►) EXTEND FROM "STAGE" TO WALLS OF ROOM.

NOTE: "SLITS" ARE ALWAYS IN EXACT CENTER OF PAINTED ARCHES. FOR MORE INFORMATION REFER TO SECTION OF TEXT ON PAINTING.

FOR MORE INFORMATION ABOUT WALL FRAGMENT, WELL, AND "BOXES + CRATES" SEE SECTION OF TEXT ON CONSTRUCTION.

HE THAT SHOULD COME

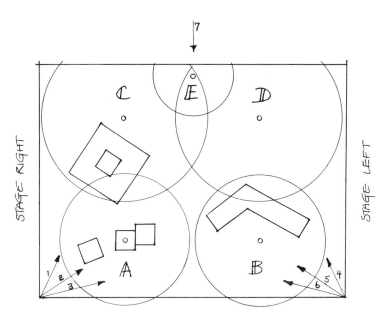

LIGHT PLOT:

LIGHT	LOCATED	AIMED AT	COLOR
1	STAGE RT.	C	S. PINK, 841
2	"	A & D	B. AMBER, 802
3	"	B	" "
4	STAGE LFT.	D	ST. BLUE, 854
5	"	B & C	S. PINK, 841
6	"	A	ST. BLUE, 854
7	BK. STAGE CEN.	ARCH	NO GEL

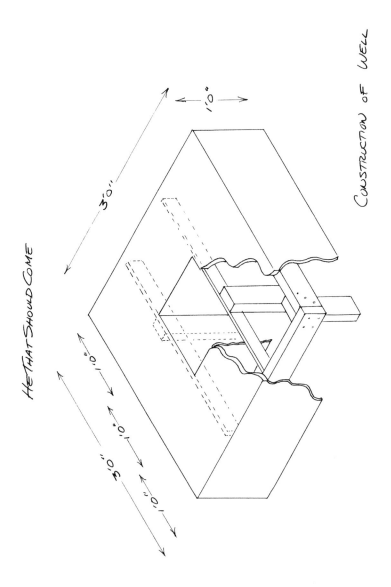

He That Should Come

3'0"

5'0"

1'0"

1'0"

1'0"

1'0"

Construction of Well

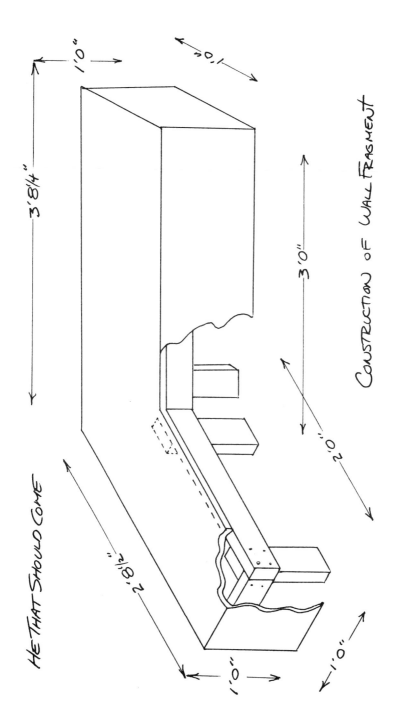

He That Should Come

Construction of Wall Fragment

1'0"

1'0"

3'8¼"

3'0"

2'0"

2'8½"

1'0"

1'0"

SKETCH SHOWING HOW STAGE LEFT CORNER POSTS ARE CONSTRUCTED IN REVERSE.

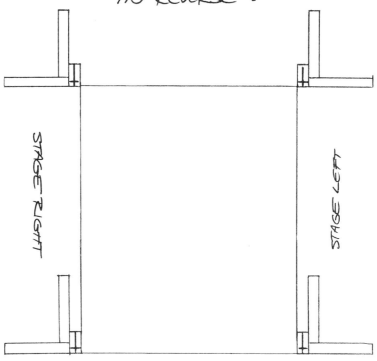

STAGE RIGHT

STAGE LEFT

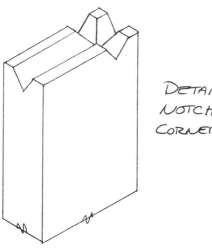

DETAIL OF NOTCHES IN CORNERPOST

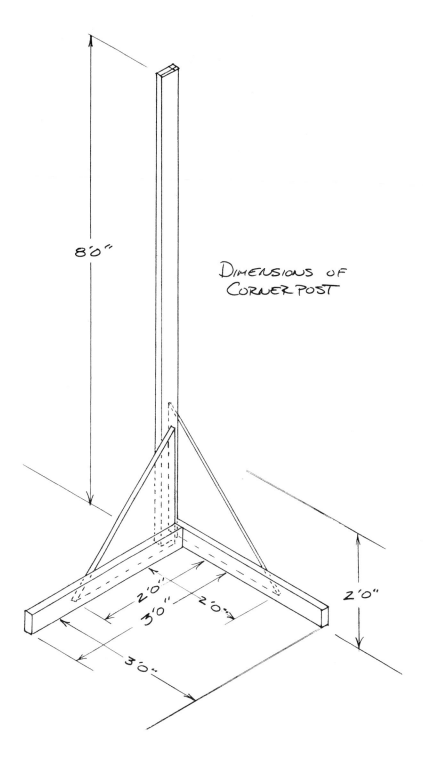

8'0"

DIMENSIONS OF
CORNER POST

2'0"

2'0"

2'0"

3'0"

3'0"

OTHER VINEYARD TITLES

CELTIC INVOCATIONS by Alexander Carmichael. Collected in the Highlands and Islands of Scotland, these ancient prayers were preserved for many centuries in the oral tradition and threads of pre-Christian beliefs were woven comfortably into the cloth of a living Christian faith. Perhaps no other spirituality has shown such a strong yet simple sense of God's presence in the world. The Celtic Christians seldom left the spiritual behind in the living of their lives nor the world behind in their prayers. Illustrated with Celtic initials. $5.95 in paper.

A BOOK OF HOURS by Elizabeth Yates with art by Carol Aymar Armstrong. Like and unlike Medieval Books of Hours, Yates' A BOOK OF HOURS embraces the ordinariness of everyday life and finds it holy. Delicate leaf prints decorate each page in soft red or slate blue. $2.95 in paper. $5.95 in cloth.

DOORWAY TO MEDITATION by Avery Brooke with art by Robert Pinart. Explains and defines Christian meditation with great clarity. Seldom have art and theology been so blended. A gift book, yet used as a text from high school through seminary. $4.95 in paper.

HOW TO MEDITATE WITHOUT LEAVING THE WORLD. Sequel to the above, this is a step by step description of how you may learn and/or teach Christian meditation. Illustrated by many anecdotes told with charm and warmth. $3.95 in paper.

ROOTS OF SPRING edited by Avery Brooke with art by Robert Pinart. A narrative anthology of love, hope and commitment. Superb pen drawings. "As beautiful a work of its kind as I have ever seen." Davie Napier. $4.95 in paper.

COOKING WITH CONSCIENCE by Alice Benjamin and Harriett Corrigan. A book for people concerned about world hunger. For those who shop in supermarkets, a nutritionally sound introduction to vegetarian cooking, explained in the simplest terms. $2.00 in paper.

AS NEVER BEFORE by Avery Brooke with photographs by Alex Darrow and students of the Wykeham-Gunnery Schools. If our world were coming to an end, what should we do? "A very quiet, simple, beautiful, and theologically sound answer . . . Stunning photographs of a New England spring." *The New Review of Books and Religion.* $5.95 in cloth.

Vineyard Books may be obtained from your bookstore or send check to Vineyard Books, Inc., Box 3315, Noroton, Conn. 06820. Add 50¢ postage and handling for each book.